英文
日本 絵 とき事典 3
ILLUSTRATED
EATING IN JAPAN
［飲食編］

About This Book

1) Layout

The book is in ten parts, and each of them contains a number of short illustrated articles which
can be read in any order, either for enjoyment,
or, using the index at the back of the book, for
reference.

2) Lettering

All Japanese words that appear in this book are
in the Hepburn System of Romanization and as
a general rule, when they appear in the text
they are in italics. (However, this does not apply
to headings and bold type.)
In addition, long vowels have a solid line above
(Ex. *Tōfu*) and e's at the end of words which
are pronounced have accents above (Ex. Saké).

Dear Readers,

There is a saying "To know a country is to eat the food of the country." Food reflects the national character, taste preference, view towards seasons, aesthetic sense, life-style, etc. of a country. Therefore it is said that cooking is culture.

Starting with 'sushi', 'tempura' and 'sukiyaki', regional delicacies and local dishes are widely introduced in this book. Confections, 'sakê', and tea are also introduced, besides cooking. Go for a taste and culture tour of Japan through this book and enjoy it to your heart's content.

We hope that readers will find this volume, along with its sister volumes 'A LOOK INTO JAPAN' and 'LIVING JAPANESE STYLE', an easily-read and insightful guide into "EATING IN JAPAN".

CONTENTS

Traditional Cuisine 51

Rice Dishes & Pickles 71

Noodle Dishes 89

Seasonal & Regional Cooking 99

Confectionery & Drinks 127

Ingredients & Seasonings 147

A Few Simple Recipes 161

Supplement 173

COLUMN

JAPANESE SOUP

APPEARANCE OF RESTAURANTS

There are the restaurants specializing in 'sushi', 'unagi', 'tempura', also all in one and family restaurants. If you are really interested in Japanese food we recommend the following specialty restaurants. The atmosphere of traditional Japanese style and vivid spirit of the cooks will make your visit more enjoyable.

Sushi-ya

寿司屋

The Japanese are generally very fond of *sushi; sushi-ya (sushi* restaurants) can be found all over the country, and almost all *sushi* restaurants operate the "meals-on-wheels" service known as *demaé* (see p.74). The price and quality of *sushi* vary greatly from restaurant to restaurant.

All *sushi-ya* have a *noren* (half-curtain) hanging outside with the restaurant's name on. The restaurant is open when the *noren* is out, and closed when it is taken in.

At the counter in *sushi* restaurants, you can order individually. There aren't any particular rules for ordering.

The most important point about the *sushi*'s *neta* (topping) is its freshness. This is why *sushi* restaurants are almost always very clean. The staff are also high-spirited and energetic.

Unagi & Dojō-ya
うなぎ・どじょう屋

Unagi (eel) and *dojō* (loach) are usually served in the same restaurant. However, many traditional restaurants specialize in one or the other as a matter of pride, wishing to concentrate on perfecting the cooking of just one of the two.

If you pass an *unagi-ya (unagi* restaurant) you will certainly notice the appetizing smell of the *unagi* being broiled over charcoal.

Dojō (loach) is natively available in summer and is dipped and broiled in a soy-based mixture. This cooking is called *kabayaki*. Loach is also used in soup with the most popular dish being *yanagawa-nabe* (see p. 41).

Ryōtei

料亭

Ryōtei are the high-class traditional restaurants where the haute cuisine of Japan is to be found. Most require reservations, and some cater only to guests introduced personally.

Ryōtei do not advertise themselves with attention-catching signs, and it is easy to overlook them as you pass by. However, their deliberately-cultivated air of discreetness and exclusivity is a mark of *'iki'*, the traditional word for chic.

Morijio
A little mound of salt at the front door of restaurants means prosperity and a welcome to customers.

The meal is served by the *nakai-san* (waitress) in a *zashiki*, or *tatami*-matted room, overlooking a Japanese-style garden.

Sukiyaki-ya

すき焼屋

Sukiyaki is a luxury dish even by Japanese standards, and *sukiyaki-ya (sukiyaki* restaurants) are more lavishly-appointed than cheaper places such as *soba-ya (soba* restaurants). Families often visit them when eating out, and they are also popular among businessmen entertaining their clients.

Many *sukiyaki* restaurants are operated by well-known meat companies.

Shabu-shabu is also served at *sukiyaki-ya.*

Some *sukiyaki* restaurants have western style tables and chairs, others have Japanese style low tables on *tatami* mat.

Soba-ya
そば屋

Soba-ya can be found all over Japan. However, the *soba* and *soba-tsuyu (soba* broth) in every restaurant taste different, since the owners all develop their own special techniques and recipes. Many *soba-ya* are *shinisé,* or family concerns that have been continued through several generations, and date from the Edo era (the 17th to the 19th century).

The distinctive characteristic of *soba-ya* is their simplicity, both inside and out.

There are always disposable chopsticks, *shichimi* (see p.94) and toothpicks on the tables.

In the Edo era, *soba-ya* doubled as *izaka-ya,* or drinking establishments. Even today, they still sell *saké* (see p.140) as an accompaniment to the food.

Tonkatsu-ya
トンカツ屋

The *tonkatsu-ya* (pork-cutlet restaurant) is probably the most common eatery to be found in Japan. They are very popular places for *salaryman* (white-collar salaried workers) to have their lunch.

A good *tonkatsu-ya* fries the *ton-katsu* freshly to order.

Besides the regular *tonkatsu,* most *tonkatsu-ya* also offer *korokké* (fried croquettes), *furai* (seafood, vegetables, etc., fried in batter), and *kushi-agé* (pork, chicken, seafood, vegetables, etc., fried on skewers).

Numerous *yakitori-ya (yakitori* restaurants) can be found in any entertainment district. Many advertise themselves by hanging a large red paper lantern called *aka-chōchin* outside. The *aka-chōchin* is also used by other drinking and eating establishments, and the word *"aka-chōchin"* itself has become the term used to describe such establishments.

The deliciously enticing aroma of chicken being grilled titillates the nostrils as one approaches a *yakitori-ya*.

Yakitori

In the evening after work, *yakitori-ya* fill up with *sararīman* (white-collar company employees) stopping off for a drink, a snack, and a chat before going home.

Okonomiyaki-ya
お好み焼屋

Okonomiyaki-ya (okonomiyaki restaurants) are most popular in the Kansai region in the west of Japan, but there are also many in Tōkyō and other cities in the Kantō region.

Okonomiyaki

Beer, whisky, and other alcoholic drinks are also available.

Order your favorite ingredients from the à la carte menu and cook the *okonomiyaki* yourself.

Oden-ya

おでん屋

Specialty *oden-ya (oden* restaurants) serve *oden* all the year round, but most *yakitori-ya (yakitori* restaurants) and *izaka-ya* (cheap drinking and eating places) serve it only in winter.

Most *oden-ya* are so small that they are easily missed and have to be searched out carefully.

Oden

At an *oden-ya,* the *oden* is kept bubbling in a pot and you can order your *ganmo-doki* (fried *tōfu,* see p.149), *hanpen*(fish cake, see p. 154), etc., à la carte.

Department-store Restaurant
デパートの食堂

All department stores have at least one large restaurant. Most ordinary restaurants specialize in a particular type of food, but department-store restaurants serve a variety of food which can include Japanese, Western, and Chinese. Most of the foods described in this book can be found at these restaurants.

Department-store restaurants often have large show-windows displaying colorful wax models of the food.

Department-store restaurants are good for families because it is easy for everyone to order their favorite dish.

DINING IN JAPAN

Where to Eat

You'll be able to eat decent traditional Japanese food even at inexpensive restaurants. The restaurants shown in chapter 1 of this book are recommended. A *ryōtei* is a rather expensive restaurant, so you'd better get price information beforehand. When you go to a *sushi* restaurant for the first time, telling the *sushi* cook your budget at first or ordering a set menu is recommended.

How to Eat

At general restaurants, in case waiters or waitresses don't take you to a seat, take any available seat. There aren't any rules for ordering food, but state clearly what you want. When you don't know how to call the dish you want to eat, say *"Aré o kudasai"* pointing to the dish which somebody else is eating.

DINING OUT

Let us introduce
dishes to dine out with.
'Sushi', 'tempura', 'sukiyaki'
are famous in other countries
too, also 'nabemono' is in the
hearts of the Japanese people.
Other unique dishes are
recommended as well.

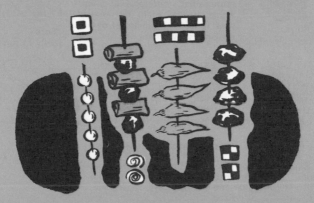

Nigirizushi is also known as *edomaézushi*, from the fact that the original ingredients were caught in the bay in front *(maé)* of old Tōkyō (Edo). Originally, *sushi* was a popular food sold from the mobile stalls known as *yatai* (see p.124). It appealed to the busy people of Edo because it was quick to prepare, and they were not kept waiting after ordering.

Sushi ordered à la carte is served in pairs. There are many other kinds, such as *hiramé* (flounder), *ika* (squid), *tako* (octopus), *kohada* (punctatus), *hotategai* (scallop), *aoyagi* (trough shell) and *tamago-yaki* (sweet egg omelette) besides the ones shown here.

Ikura
(salmon roe)

Toro
(belly of tuna)

Uni
(sea urchin roe)

Anago
(conger eel)

Akagai
(ark shell)

Ebi
(prawn)

HOW TO MAKE NIGIRIZUSHI

1) Squeeze some *sushi-meshi* (rice seasoned with vinegar, sugar and salt) into a bite-sized oblong.

2) Press the *tané* (topping) onto the rice with two fingers.

Neta (topping)

3) Shape and serve.

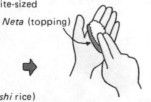

Sushi-meshi (sushi rice)

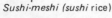

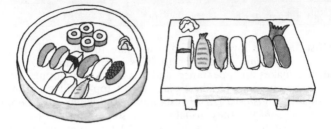

Sushi can either be ordered à la carte or as a set. Sets usually come in three grades, *tokujō* (extra-special), *jō* (special) and *nami* (regular) depending on the price of the ingredients included. Sets usually include a selection of *nigirizushi* and *makizushi* (roll *sushi*) and are served in individual lacquer bowls or on small wooden trays with legs.

Saikuzasa

Saikuzasa are the artistically-cut leaves of *sasa* (bamboo grass) used to decorate the food.

Sushi is dipped in soy sauce before being eaten. *Sushi* can be eaten with chopsticks or picked up with the fingers.

Agari

The green tea served with *sushi* comes in a large cup called a *yunomijawan* and is known as *agari*.

Gari

The vinegared thinly-sliced ginger known in *sushi* terminology as *gari* is used to refresh the palate between different items of *sushi*.

Most Japanese love fish, and many like to eat it raw, in the form of *sashimi*. Whenever there is a party, *sashimi* almost always makes an appearance, and it is also a very popular form of home cooking. The best place to get top-quality *sashimi* is probably a *sushi-ya (sushi* restaurant), and when most people go to a *sushi-ya,* they usually order some *sashimi* first as an hors d'oeuvre with their drinks, and later order *nigiri* as the meal proper.

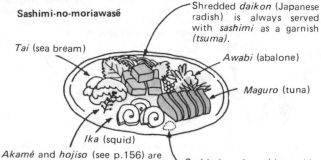

Sashimi-no-moriawasé

Tai (sea bream)

Shredded *daikon* (Japanese radish) is always served with *sashimi* as a garnish *(tsuma).*

Awabi (abalone)

Maguro (tuna)

Ika (squid)

Akamé and *hojiso* (see p.156) are two plants often used as garnishes in Japanese cooking. They are known as *yakumi* for their medicinal properties.

Sashimi and *sushi* would not be complete without *wasabi* (Japanese horse-radish).

Sugata-zukuri

The Japanese have traditionally considered it auspicious, as well as being more natural, to serve fish complete with head and tail. *Sashimi* served in this way is called *sugata-zukuri*.

Chirashizushi
散らし寿司

Chirashizushi consists of *sashimi* and other ingredients arranged on top of *sushi* rice in a bowl. Since it is easy to prepare, it is a popular dish for eating at home. Cooked items such as *kamaboko*, *denbu*, and *shiitakē* are used as well as raw fish.

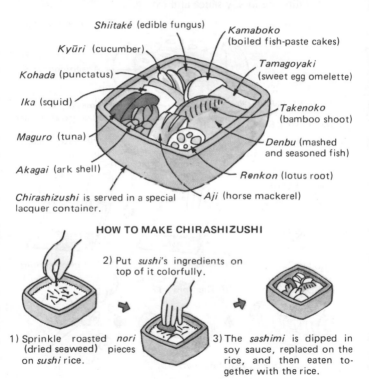

Shiitakē (edible fungus)

Kyūri (cucumber)

Kohada (punctatus)

Ika (squid)

Maguro (tuna)

Akagai (ark shell)

Kamaboko (boiled fish-paste cakes)

Tamagoyaki (sweet egg omelette)

Takenoko (bamboo shoot)

Denbu (mashed and seasoned fish)

Renkon (lotus root)

Aji (horse mackerel)

Chirashizushi is served in a special lacquer container.

HOW TO MAKE CHIRASHIZUSHI

1) Sprinkle roasted *nori* (dried seaweed) pieces on *sushi* rice.

2) Put *sushi*'s ingredients on top of it colorfully.

3) The *sashimi* is dipped in soy sauce, replaced on the rice, and then eaten together with the rice.

25

Makizushi is made by spreading some *sushi* rice on top of a sheet of *nori* (dried seaweed) on a bamboo mat called a *makisu*, then placing seafood, vegetables, etc., on top of the rice and rolling the whole thing up tightly. The roll is then cut into sections for dipping in soy sauce and eating.

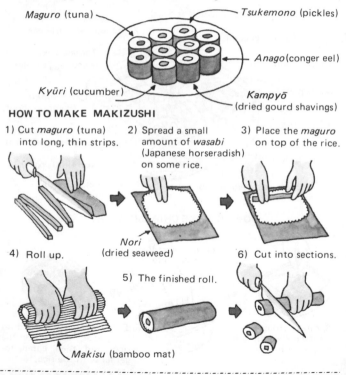

Maguro (tuna)

Tsukemono (pickles)

Anago (conger eel)

Kyūri (cucumber)

Kampyō (dried gourd shavings)

HOW TO MAKE MAKIZUSHI

1) Cut *maguro* (tuna) into long, thin strips.

2) Spread a small amount of *wasabi* (Japanese horseradish) on some rice.

3) Place the *maguro* on top of the rice.

Nori (dried seaweed)

4) Roll up.

5) The finished roll.

6) Cut into sections.

Makisu (bamboo mat)

Temakizushi
手巻き寿司

Temakizushi is similar to *makizushi* except that it is rolled into a cone shape in the hand instead of into a cylindrical shape in a *makisu*. It is easy to make and in fact was invented by amateur *sushi* chefs at home, being adopted by proper *sushi* restaurants later.

Kyūri (cucumber)

Maguro (tuna)

Nattō (fermented soy beans)

HOW TO MAKE TEMAKIZUSHI

1) Place some *sushi* rice on top of some *nori* (dried seaweed).

2) Place a *shiso* (beefsteak plant) leaf and some *nattō* on the rice.

Nori

Nattō

Shiso

3) Roll up.

4) The finished *temaki*.

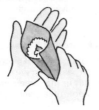

Sukiyaki
すき焼

The Japanese only started eating meat regularly at the end of the last century. Since people were unused to meat, it first became popularized in the form of *nabemono* (hotpot), a style of cooking which suited the Japanese taste. *Sukiyaki* is probably the best-known Japanese meat dish and is often cooked and eaten at home, but it is still regarded as something of a luxury.

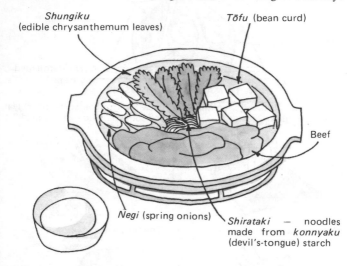

Shungiku (edible chrysanthemum leaves)

Tōfu (bean curd)

Beef

Negi (spring onions)

Shirataki — noodles made from *konnyaku* (devil's-tongue) starch

The Flavor Differences between Kantō and Kansai

There are two different ways of cooking *sukiyaki*, in Kansai district (Kyōto - Ōsaka area), they cook the meat first seasoning with soy sauce and sugar, and eat it, then cook the vegetables in the same sauce as the meat. In Kantō district (Tōkyō area), they cook meat, vegetables, and *shirataki* altogether adding the *warishita*.

HOW TO COOK SUKIYAKI

The *nabé* (pot) used for cooking *sukiyaki* is usually thick and shallow, and made of iron.

To cook *sukiyaki*, first cook the meat a little, then add the *warishita*, vegetables, and *shirataki* and boil them all up together.

Warishita

The stock in which *sukiyaki* is cooked is called *warishita*. It contains a high proportion of sugar, *mirin* and soy sauce, giving it a sweet, spicy taste.

Sukiyaki is cooked at the table and is dipped in a beaten raw egg before being eaten.

29

Shabu-shabu
しゃぶ しゃぶ

Shabu-shabu is a popular Japanese meat dish, similar to *suki-yaki*, consisting of thinly-sliced beef (about 1 mm. thick) and vegetables dipped in boiling stock and eaten with special sauces. There is also a version of *shabu-shabu* using crab, called *kani-shabu*.

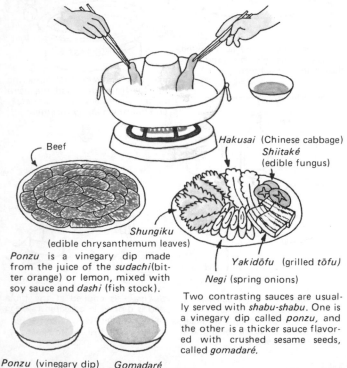

Beef

Hakusai (Chinese cabbage)
Shiitaké (edible fungus)

Shungiku (edible chrysanthemum leaves)

Ponzu is a vinegary dip made from the juice of the *sudachi* (bitter orange) or lemon, mixed with soy sauce and *dashi* (fish stock).

Yakidōfu (grilled *tōfu*)

Negi (spring onions)

Two contrasting sauces are usually served with *shabu-shabu*. One is a vinegary dip called *ponzu*, and the other is a thicker sauce flavored with crushed sesame seeds, called *gomadaré*.

Ponzu (vinegary dip) *Gomadaré*

Yosé-nabé is a rich hotpot dish containing an assortment of seafood, vegetables, and chicken. It appears on the menus of many different kinds of restaurant in the winter, and is also a popular dish for cooking at home.

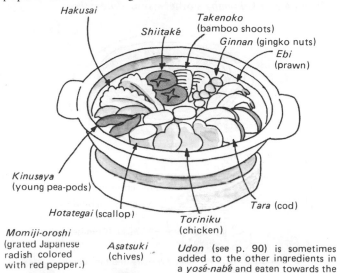

Hakusai

Shiitaké

Takenoko
(bamboo shoots)

Ginnan (gingko nuts)

Ebi
(prawn)

Kinusaya
(young pea-pods)

Tara (cod)

Hotategai (scallop)

Toriniku
(chicken)

Momiji-oroshi
(grated Japanese
radish colored
with red pepper.)

Asatsuki
(chives)

Udon (see p. 90) is sometimes added to the other ingredients in a *yosé-nabé* and eaten towards the end of the meal.

The broth of *yosé-nabé* is full flavored just by itself, so it is not necessary to add anything else, but usually a small amount of spicy vegetables are added as condiments.

Kaki-nabé

かき鍋

Kaki-nabé (oyster hotpot) differs from other *nabemono* in that the stock is flavored with *miso*. The *miso* is spread around the rim of the pot, looking like an earth embankment *(doté)*, and is scraped off with chopsticks as the *nabé* is cooked. This is the origin of *kaki-nabé*'s other name, *doté-nabé*.

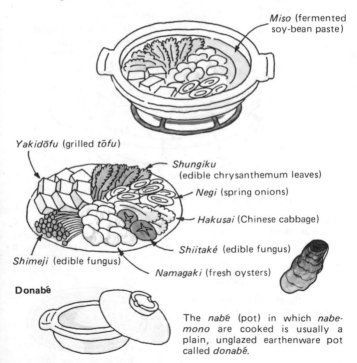

Miso (fermented soy-bean paste)

Yakidōfu (grilled *tōfu*)

Shungiku (edible chrysanthemum leaves)

Negi (spring onions)

Hakusai (Chinese cabbage)

Shiitaké (edible fungus)

Shimeji (edible fungus)

Namagaki (fresh oysters)

Donabé

The *nabé* (pot) in which *nabemono* are cooked is usually a plain, unglazed earthenware pot called *donabé*.

Chanko-nabé
ちゃんこ鍋

Chanko-nabé, the staple diet of *sumō* wrestlers, is a nourishment-packed hotpot consisting of seafood, vegetables, meat, and anything else the cook cares to put in. The stock can be flavored with soy sauce, *miso*, *sakekasu* (*saké lees*) or other seasonings.

Potatoes

Chicken on the bone

Carrot

Tōfu

Negi (spring onions)

Shimeji
(edible fungus)

Shiitaké
(edible fungus)

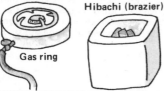

Hibachi (brazier)

Gas ring

Since *nabemono* are cooked and eaten at the table, a gas or electric ring that can be used on the dining table is a must. Many of these are portable, and the old-style ones using charcoal are still available.

Ankō-nabé
あんこう鍋

The *ankō* (angler fish) is a deep-sea fish caught only in winter. It is used complete with skin and liver in a soy sauce-based hot-pot called *ankō-nabé* and in a version of *miso-shiru (miso* soup).

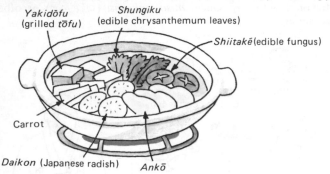

Yakidōfu (grilled *tōfu*)

Shungiku (edible chrysanthemum leaves)

Shiitaké (edible fungus)

Carrot

Daikon (Japanese radish)

Ankō

The liver of the angler fish, called *ankimo,* is said by many *saké*-lovers to be the best possible accompaniment to the drink. It is boiled and served in a dressing made from vinegar and *miso*.

Ankimo

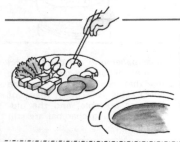

When cooking *nabemono*, hard-to-cook ingredients or those that release a lot of liquid such as fish, prawns, and *shimeji* (edible fungus) should be put in the pot first. *Tōfu* and *shungiku* should be added last.

Oden
おでん

Oden consists of a variety of ingredients such as *gammodoki* (see p.149), *konnyaku* and *tōfu* boiled for many hours in *kombu* (kelp) stock. Other types of *nabemono* are cooked and eaten on the spot, but *oden* takes a long time, since it tastes best if the ingredients are thoroughly permeated by the soy sauce-based stock.

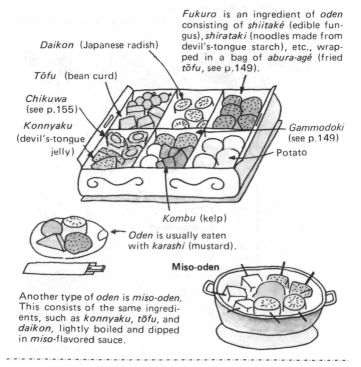

Fukuro is an ingredient of *oden* consisting of *shiitaké* (edible fungus), *shirataki* (noodles made from devil's-tongue starch), etc., wrapped in a bag of *abura-agé* (fried *tōfu*, see p.149).

Daikon (Japanese radish)

Tōfu (bean curd)

Chikuwa (see p.155)

Konnyaku (devil's-tongue jelly)

Gammodoki (see p.149)

Potato

Kombu (kelp)

Oden is usually eaten with *karashi* (mustard).

Miso-oden

Another type of *oden* is *miso-oden*. This consists of the same ingredients, such as *konnyaku*, *tōfu*, and *daikon*, lightly boiled and dipped in *miso*-flavored sauce.

Tempura
天ぷら

The origin of the word *"tempura"* is unclear, although it is most probably a corruption of a Portuguese word, since this style of cooking was introduced into Japan by Portuguese missionaries in the late 16th century. It became popularized towards the 19th century, when it was sold from the street stalls known as *yatai* (see p.124). It is now eaten in restaurants, *tempura* stalls having gone out of fashion, but it can still be bought at food counters in shops and department stores for taking home.

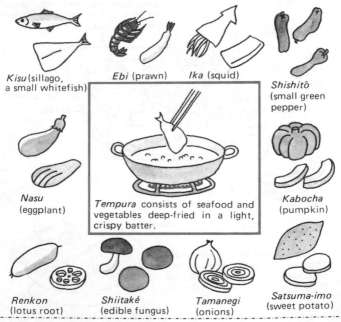

Kisu (sillago, a small whitefish)

Ebi (prawn)

Ika (squid)

Shishitō (small green pepper)

Nasu (eggplant)

Tempura consists of seafood and vegetables deep-fried in a light, crispy batter.

Kabocha (pumpkin)

Renkon (lotus root)

Shiitaké (edible fungus)

Tamanegi (onions)

Satsuma-imo (sweet potato)

Tempura can either be ordered as a set meal (*teishoku*) or à la carte. The set meal consists of an assortment of *tempura* with plain white rice, *miso-shiru* (*miso* soup) and pickles.

Oroshi-shōga
(grated ginger)

Daikon-oroshi
(grated Japanese radish)

Most *tempura* is eaten after being dipped in the soy sauce-based sauce called *tentsuyu* that is usually served with it, although eating it with salt and a wedge of lemon is also popular. If *tentsuyu* is served, the *oroshi-shōga* and *daikon-oroshi* accompanying it should be mixed into it first.

HOW TO MAKE KOROMO (BATTER)

1) Cover with flour

2) Mix egg and water.

3) Dip rapidly in the egg-and-water mixture.

Fugu
ふぐ

Fugu (swellfish) is caught in winter only, and the various *fugu* dishes that make their appearance in this season are a treat that *fugu* connoisseurs look forward to. Japanese cooking is generally renowned for its artistry, and one of the most beautiful of Japanese dishes is a large circular plate of carefully-arranged *fugusashi* (raw *fugu*) sliced almost transparently thin.

Fugusashi

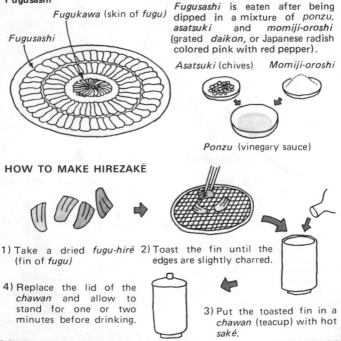

Fugukawa (skin of *fugu*)

Fugusashi

Fugusashi is eaten after being dipped in a mixture of *ponzu, asatsuki* and *momiji-oroshi* (grated *daikon,* or Japanese radish colored pink with red pepper).

Asatsuki (chives)   *Momiji-oroshi*

Ponzu (vinegary sauce)

HOW TO MAKE HIREZAKÉ

1) Take a dried *fugu-hiré* (fin of *fugu*)

2) Toast the fin until the edges are slightly charred.

3) Put the toasted fin in a *chawan* (teacup) with hot *saké.*

4) Replace the lid of the *chawan* and allow to stand for one or two minutes before drinking.

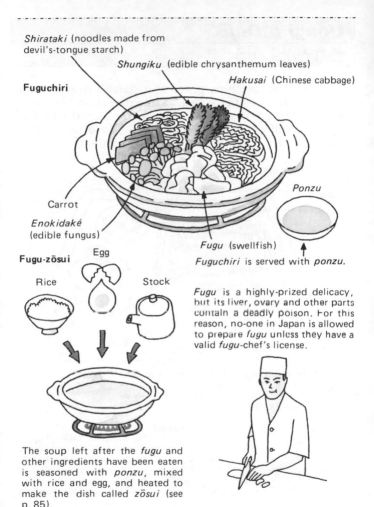

Fuguchiri

Shirataki (noodles made from devil's-tongue starch)

Shungiku (edible chrysanthemum leaves)

Hakusai (Chinese cabbage)

Carrot

Enokidaké (edible fungus)

Fugu (swellfish)

Ponzu

Fuguchiri is served with *ponzu*.

Fugu-zōsui

Rice

Egg

Stock

Fugu is a highly-prized delicacy, but its liver, ovary and other parts contain a deadly poison. For this reason, no-one in Japan is allowed to prepare *fugu* unless they have a valid *fugu*-chef's license.

The soup left after the *fugu* and other ingredients have been eaten is seasoned with *ponzu*, mixed with rice and egg, and heated to make the dish called *zōsui* (see p. 85).

Unagi (eel) has long been prized as a stamina-giving food in Japan, and the traditional custom of eating it on *"Doyō-no-ushi-no-hi"* (the Day of the Ox, during the hottest period of summer) is still said to be an effective way of avoiding heat exhaustion. *Unagi,* which is quite an expensive food, is also said to possess aphrodisiac properties. *Dojō* (loach) is a fish of a slightly lower class.

Unajū

Tsukemono (pickles)

kimosui

One of the most popular *unagi* dishes is *unajū,* which consists of *kabayaki* (charcoal-broiled eels) on top of rice in a lacquer box, with a soy sauce-based sauce.

Kabayaki

To make eel *kabayaki*, the *unagi* is cut into two fillets, brushd with a thick soy-based sauce, skewered, and broiled over charcoal, giving off a delicious aroma.

Kashirayaki and Kimoyaki

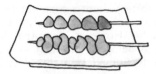

Sometimes the *kashira* (head) and *kimo* (liver) of the eel are skewered and broiled in *kabayaki* fashion.

Sanshō

Sanshō (Japanese pepper) is the light-green powdery spice invariably served with *unagi* and *dojō*.

Dojō-nabé

Dojō-nabé is a *nabemono* (hotpot) containing *dojō*, which are put in the pot live.

Kimosui

Unagi is usually served with a clear, salty soup (*suimono,* see p. 70) containing the eel's liver, which has a rather bitter taste but is said to be very nutritious.

Yanagawa-nabé

This is a very popular *dojō* dish in which the *dojō* are boiled with *gobō* (burdock root) in a sweet, spicy stock, and served in a flat earthenware dish with cooked egg on the top. *Yanagawa-nabé* is probably the easiest and most appetizing way to eat *dojō*.

Suppon (snapping turtle) is not a common dish in Japan, and is eaten only by a relatively small number of aficionados. However, those that do like it swear by it as being an excellent source of stamina and vitality. Some restaurants specialize in the full *suppon* meal, *suppon* from start to finish.

Suppon-nabé

Negi (spring onions)

Tōfu (bean curd)

Enokidaké
(edible fungus)

Suppon meat

The *suppon* meat in *suppon-nabé* is of course important, but the soup, with its rich flavor derived from hours of simmering, is one of the main attractions of this dish. The soup is seasoned with soy sauce.

Tamago (eggs)

Suppon eggs are eaten as they are or mixed with the blood.

Ikichi (blood from the live *suppon*)

The blood of the live *suppon* is mixed with wine or *saké* and drunk for its revitalizing and aphrodisiac properties.

Suimono

Suppon is also used to make *suimono* (clear soup), *nimono* (stew), *yakimono* (a grilled dish), etc.

Along with *korokké* (croquettes), *tonkatsu* (fried breaded pork cutlet) is one of the most popular Western foods in Japan, and has now become thoroughly Japanized.

The difference between *tonkatsu* and the Western cutlet is the temperature at which they are fried. *Tonkatsu* is fried slowly at a temperature of about 160°C.

An indispensable adjunct to *tonkatsu* is the sauce, a thick version of Worcester sauce. Each restaurant goes to great pains to develop its own unique flavors.

Tonkatsu Sauce

*Miso-shiru
(miso* soup)

Karashı (mustard)

Rice

Tonkatsu is almost always served with a pile of shredded cabbage and some mustard.

Korokké
コロッケ

Croquettes were first introduced into Japan in the end of 19th century, and the popular dish known as *korokké* is an adaptation of this originally Western dish to the Japanese taste. It consists of stir-fried minced meat and chopped onions mixed with mashed potato and fried in breadcrumbs.

HOW TO MAKE KOROKKÉ

1) Mash some boiled potatoes.

6) Fry in oil at 180°C until golden-brown.

2) Stir-fry minced meat and chopped onions.

5) Dip first in flour, then in beaten egg, and finally in breadcrumbs.

3) Mix the meat and onions with the mashed potato.

4) Shape into an oval.

There is a wide variation of croquette in taste and shape, such as;

Kani-kurīmu-korokké

Crab

White sauce

Mīto-korokké

Meat

Karē-korokké
(curry-flavored *korokké*)

Korokké are served with **rice**, in curry-flavored sauce, between slices of bread, and in various other ways. They are the most popular item at the take-away fried-food counters of local butchers' shops.

Korokké-karē (*korokké* with curry-flavored sauce)

Korokké

Korokké-bāgā (*korokké* in a bun)

Kushikatsu

Kushikatsu is another fried item that rivals *korokké* in popularity. It consists of pork and *Tamanegi* (onions) fried on skewers.

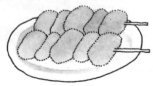

Yakitori

焼き鳥

Yakitori consists of various parts of the chicken grilled on bamboo skewers over charcoal. It is flavored during cooking either with a sour-sweet soy-based sauce or with salt alone. *Yakitori* is one of the most popular and well-known Japanese foods.

The flavor of the sauce (*taré*) brushed onto the *yakitori* during cooking is very important, and the chefs of each *yakitori-ya* (*yakitori* pub) spend a long time getting it just how they want it.

Yakitori is usually eaten with two kinds of peppery spice, *ichimi* (red pepper, see p.160) and *shichimi* (see p. 94).

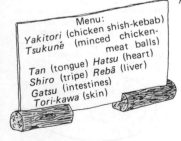

Menu:
Yakitori (chicken shish-kebab)
Tsukune (minced chicken-meat balls)

Tan (tongue) *Hatsu* (heart)
Shiro (tripe) *Rebā* (liver)
Gatsu (intestines)
Tori-kawa (skin)

Chicken

Negi (spring onions)

Kushi-agé

串揚げ

Kushi-agé consists of seafood and vegetables on small bamboo skewers, dipped in flour, egg, and breadcrumbs and fried in the same way as *tonkatsu* (see p.43). Many restaurants specialize entirely in this style of cooking.

Shiitaké
(edible fungus)

Uzura-tamago
(quail's egg)

Ebi (prawn)

Beef

Piman
(green bell pepper)

Shishitō
(small green pepper)

Hotategai
(scallop)

Ika (squid)

Kushi-agé is usually served with lemon slices and a sauce that is a specialty of the particular restaurant.

Robata-yaki

炉端焼

The *robata-yaki*-style pub is a relatively new invention recrea ting the homely atmosphere and plain cooking of an old-style country farmhouse (*robata* means "hearthside"). All kinds of fish, vegetables and other dishes are available, and the cooks grill the food over charcoal in front of the customers.

A Typical Robata-yaki Dish

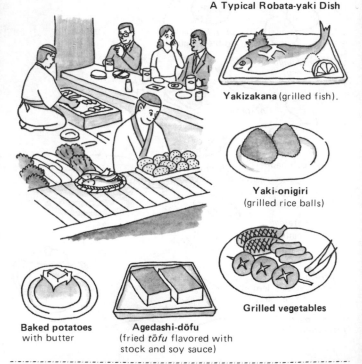

Yakizakana (grilled fish).

Yaki-onigiri
(grilled rice balls)

Grilled vegetables

Baked potatoes
with butter

Agedashi-dōfu
(fried *tōfu* flavored with stock and soy sauce)

Okonomiyaki
お好み焼

Okonomiyaki is a type of pancake whose name literally means "cook to taste". At an *okonomiyaki* restaurant, as the name implies, the customers select the ingredients from the menu and cook the pancakes themselves, on a hot plate set in the center of the table.

Mix the ingredients together well with chopsticks.

Flour

Water

Egg

Pork

Shredded cabbage

Ika (squid)

Ebi (prawn)

Tenkasu
(also called *agedama*, small pieces of fried *tempura* batter)

Pour the mixture onto the *teppan* and cook it on both sides. When it is ready, brush it thickly with *okonomiyaki* sauce, sprinkle it with *aonori* and cut it into small pieces and enjoy it.

Okonomiyaki sauce

Aonori (dried seaweed flakes)

Teppan (hotplate)

Aburahiki (oil brush)

Yakiniku
焼き肉

Many restaurants in Japan specialize in *yakiniku* (grilled meat), originally a Korean dish. Meat and offal marinated in a spicy dip are grilled on a hot plate at the table and dipped in a spicy Korean-style sauce before being eaten. This form of cooking is also popular at home.

Taré

The *taré*, or sauce, with which *yakiniku* is eaten consists of *miso* (fermented soy-bean paste) spiced with *tōgarashi* (red pepper).

Kimuchi

Kimuchi (kim chee) is a very hot Korean pickle containing red pepper. It is made with *hakusai* (Chinese cabbage), *kyūri* (cucumber) or other vegetables.

Bibimba

This is Korean-style *mazé-gohan* (boiled rice mixed with vegetables and other ingredients). It consists of a bowl of rice with *mamé-moyashi* (bean sprouts), *zenmai* (flowering fern), minced meat and other ingredients on top. All the ingredients should be mixed together well with chopsticks before being eaten.

TRADITIONAL CUISINE

Traditional Japanese
cuisine is mostly connected
with annual events and religion,
which expresses the seasons and
aesthetic sense. These artistic
dishes are worth trying.

Kaiseki-ryōri is a highly-refined style of cooking which originated in the art of the tea ceremony, *sadō*. It was felt that a light repast before the ceremony itself would increase the guests' enjoyment of the tea. In keeping with the spirit of the tea ceremony, *kaiseki-ryōri* is simple and artistic, and embodies the Japanese concepts of *wabi* (simplicity and quietness) and *sabi* (unstudied elegance). Some restaurants specialize in *kaiseki-ryōri*, and it is also served at the traditional Japanese restaurants known as *ryōtei*.

FULL KAISEKI COURSE:

Matcha (powdered green tea)

Yutō (hot water with scorched rice)

Yakimono (grilled fish)

Hashiarai (delicate soup)

Mukōzuké (side dish, usually raw seafood)

Shiizakana (accompaniment to *saké*)

Wanmori (main dish, meat or fish with vegetables and garnishes in clear soup)

Meshi (rice)

Shiru (*miso* soup)

Hassun (various delicacies on a square tray)

Kaiseki has its own special etiquette for the serving of the food by the host or hostess and its reception by the guests. Manners are of course important when eating other kinds of Japanese food, but they are emphasized even more than usual in *kaiseki-ryōri*.

Meshi (rice)

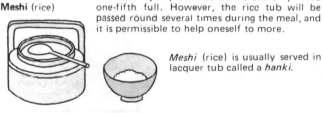

In *kaiseki-ryōri*, the rice bowls are only filled one-fifth full. However, the rice tub will be passed round several times during the meal, and it is permissible to help oneself to more.

Meshi (rice) is usually served in a lacquer tub called a *hanki*.

Shirumono

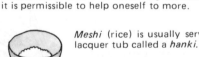

The *miso* used to make the *miso-shiru* in *kaiseki-ryōri* is usually *shiro-miso* (white *miso*) with a low salt content. It is served in small portions like the rice, but the guests can help themselves to seconds if they wish.

Saké

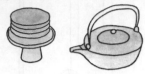

This dish usually consists of raw white fish such as *tai* (sea bream) or *hiramé* (flounder). The *mukō-zuké* should not be touched until after the *saké* has been served.

Saké (see p.140) is served as an accompaniment to *kaiseki-ryōri*, but only to enhance the exquisiteness of the cuisine. A guest would be considered extremely ill-mannered if he or she drunk enough to become tiddly.

Mukōzuké

Wanmori

This main dish consists of meat or fish with seasonal vegetables in a delicately-flavored clear soup. The ingredients of the dish are arranged to please the eye as well as the palate.

Yakimono

This dish consists of grilled fish from which the bones have been removed to make it easy to eat.

Shiizakana

Shiizakana is a special dish served by the host or hostess as an accompaniment to *saké*. It usually consists of from one to three items such as boiled vegetables or *sunomono* (a vinegared tidbit).

Hashi-arai

Hashi-arai, literally "chopstick wash", consists of a delicately-flavored *suimono* (clear soup) served between the other dishes.

Hassun

The name of *hassun* comes from the size of the square tray on which it is served, eight *sun* by eight *sun* (one *sun* being about 3 cm); and eight *sun* in Japanese is expressed as *hassun*. This is the last of the dishes served as an accompaniment to *saké*, and it usually consists of every sort of delicacies.

Yutō and Kōnomono

The final course in *kaiseki-ryōri* is a small dish of *kōnomono* (pickles) and a wooden pitcher of hot water (*yutō*) containing *okogé* (scorched rice).

Matcha and Wagashi

When the guests have finished eating, *matcha* (powdered green tea, see p.145) and *wagashi* (Japanese cakes, see p.127) are served. *Matcha* is made from top-quality tea leaves and is always used in the tea ceremony. The correct procedure is to finish eating the *wagashi* and then to drink the *matcha*.

Shōjin-ryōri
精進料理

Shōjin-ryōri is the name given to the vegetarian food eaten by Buddhist priests as part of the asceticism that they practice in their lives. This unique style of cooking, which uses no meat, fish, or eggs, can also be enjoyed by ordinary people at temples in places such as Kyōto and Kamakura.

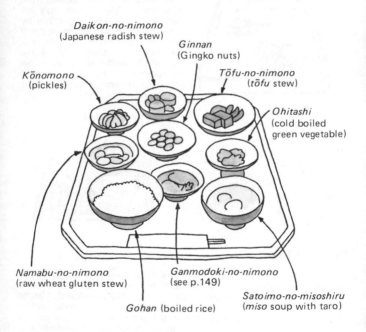

Daikon-no-nimono
(Japanese radish stew)

Ginnan
(Gingko nuts)

Kōnomono
(pickles)

Tōfu-no-nimono
(tōfu stew)

Ohitashi
(cold boiled
green vegetable)

Namabu-no-nimono
(raw wheat gluten stew)

Ganmodoki-no-nimono
(see p.149)

Gohan (boiled rice)

Satoimo-no-misoshiru
(*miso* soup with taro)

Yamatoimo-no-chawan-mushi

Chawan-mushi is normally a steamed egg custard containing vegetables, but in *shōjin-ryōri*, the egg is replaced by *yamatoimo* (a kind of yam) or *kabu* (turnip).

Namayuba-no-futomakizushi

Namayuba (see p. 148) is the protein skin that forms on *tō-nyū* (soy-bean milk) when the latter is boiled. It is used in stews and instead of the *nori* in *makizushi* (see p. 26).

Namabu-no-agemono

Namabu, or raw wheat gluten, is the protein from wheat flour left behind after the starch is removed. *Namabu,* for which Kyoto is well-known, is usually dried or toasted to make the ordinary *fu* (wheat gluten) used in some *udon* and other dishes.

Namabu is used mainly in *nimono* (boiled dishes, or stews), but it is also a tasty ingredient of some *agemono* (fried dishes).

Various Shapes of Namabu

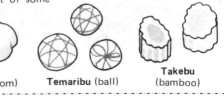

Umebu (plum blossom) **Temaribu** (ball) **Takebu** (bamboo)

Japan's original *shōjin-ryōri* was improved by the introduction of *ōbaku-ryōri*, a form of *shōjin-ryōri* from China. Some restaurants also serve *shōjin-ryōri* in the form of *kaiseki-ryōri* (see p. 52).

The *shōjin-ryōri* served in temples is cooked by the priests themselves, and it is usually necessary to make a reservation.

Kōyadōfu

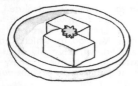

Kōyadōfu (dried *tōfu*) is an indispensable ingredient in *shōjin-ryōri* and is used in stews and fried dishes.

Dengaku

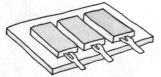

Tōfu is an important source of protein for priests or anyone else eating only *shōjin-ryōri*. *Dengaku* consists of hot baked *tōfu* coated with various *miso* sauces.

Gomadōfu

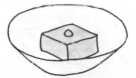

This is the most typical *shōjin-ryōri* dish. It consists of *kuzu* (arrowroot starch) flavored with ground *goma* (sesame) and has a texture somewhat similar to that of *tōfu*.

Shōjin-agé

Tempura (see p. 36) usually uses seafood as well as vegetables as its ingredients. *Shōjin-agé* is a form of *tempura* which uses vegetables only.

Osechi-ryōri
お節料理

Osechi-ryōri is the special food cooked at home to celebrate New Year, one of the most important festivals in Japan. The food itself differs from region to region and from family to family, but the associated wish for health, happiness, and a good harvest is the same everywhere.

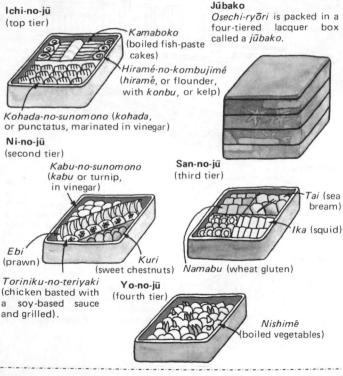

Ichi-no-jū
(top tier)

Kamaboko
(boiled fish-paste cakes)

Hiramé-no-kombujimé
(*hiramé*, or flounder, with *konbu*, or kelp)

Kohada-no-sunomono (*kohada*, or punctatus, marinated in vinegar)

Jūbako
Osechi-ryōri is packed in a four-tiered lacquer box called a *jūbako*.

Ni-no-jū
(second tier)

Kabu-no-sunomono
(*kabu* or turnip, in vinegar)

San-no-jū
(third tier)

Tai (sea bream)

Ika (squid)

Ebi
(prawn)

Kuri
(sweet chestnuts)

Namabu (wheat gluten)

Toriniku-no-teriyaki
(chicken basted with a soy-based sauce and grilled).

Yo-no-jū
(fourth tier)

Nishimē
(boiled vegetables)

Kuromamé

Black beans, a symbol of health, are boiled in syrup.

Kurikinton

Kurikinton consists of *kuri* (sweet chestnuts) and mashed *satsuma-imo* (sweet potato) boiled in a sweet sauce.

Tazukuri

Tazukuri is a symbol of a good harvest and consists of *tsukudani* (see p. 111) made with small sardines.

Kazunoko

Kazunoko (herring roe), with its myriads of tiny eggs, is a symbol of procreativity. It is usually seasoned with soy sauce.

Nishimé

This consists of artistically-arranged boiled vegetables such as carrot, *gobō* (burdock root), *renkon* (lotus root), *yatsugashira* (taro), etc.

Namasu

This is a salad of shredded *daikon* (Japanese radish) and carrot seasoned in vinegar.

OTHER NEW YEAR'S DISHES

Zōni

Mochi (rice cakes)

Kagami-mochi

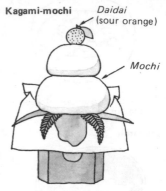

Daidai (sour orange)

Mochi

All over Japan, it is the custom on New Year's Day to eat *zōni*, a soup containing *mochi* (pounded rice cakes) together with vegetables, fish, chicken, and other ingredients. The exact ingredients, the shape of the *mochi*, and the seasoning of the soup, whether soy sauce or *miso* (fermented soybean paste), vary from region to region.

Kagami-mochi is a special *mochi* (pounded rice cake) offered to the gods at New Year. It consists of two round *mochi* — a small one sitting on top of a larger one.

Yakizakana (grilled fish)

Toso

A special drink for New Year's Day, *toso* is spiced *saké* drunk in celebration and to pray for happiness in the coming year.

The fish eaten at New Year are auspicious ones such as *saké* (salmon), *buri* (yellowtail), and *tai* (sea bream).

Mochi-tsuki — literally, "rice-cake pounding", was a custom that all households used to carry out at the end of each year, pounding the rice with a large wooden mallet in a heavy wooden tub. The busy modern Japanese now mostly order their *mochi* from the local *komé-ya* (rice shop) or use electric *mochi*-makers.

Mochi-tsuki

Mamé-mochi

Kiri-mochi

An-mochi

There are many kinds of *mochi* — *an-mochi*, containing *anko* (adzuki-bean jam), *mamé-mochi*, containing beans, *yomogi-mochi*, containing *yomogi* (mugwort) — but the most popular is the plain white *kiri-mochi*.

Nanakusa-gayu

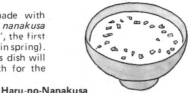

This special dish is made with *okayu* (rice gruel), and *nanakusa* (literally, "seven grasses", the first seven herbs to come out in spring). It is said that eating this dish will keep one in good health for the rest of the year.

Haru-no-Nanakusa
(*Nanakusa* in Spring)

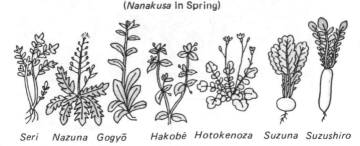

Seri   Nazuna   Gogyō   Hakobé   Hotokenoza   Suzuna   Suzushiro

Shōkadō-bentō
松花堂弁当

A *Shōkadō* is a type of container used in *kaiseki-ryōri* (see p.52); and *shōkadō-bentō* is the name given to a meal served in this container. Although it is termed *"bentō"* (boxed meal), *shōkadō-bentō* is far larger and more sumptuous than the ordinary forms of portable *bentō* and is served at the traditional Japanese restaurants known as *ryōtei* or at lunch or dinner parties. It usually contains a full range of typical Japanese dishes, from *sashimi* (raw fish) to *nimono* (boiled vegetables).

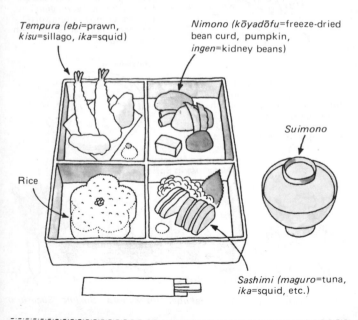

*Tempura (ebi=*prawn, *kisu=*sillago, *ika=*squid)

*Nimono (kōyadōfu=*freeze-dried bean curd, pumpkin, *ingen=*kidney beans)

Suimono

Rice

*Sashimi (maguro=*tuna, *ika=*squid, etc.)

Rice

The rice served in a *shōkadō-bentō* is usually shaped in a mould to represent a pine tree, plum blossom or cherry blossom. A seasonal decoration such as a pickled cherry blossom or *aonori* (seaweed) is placed on top of the rice.

Tempura

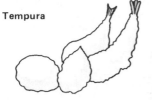

Seafood such as *ebi, ika* and *kisu,* and vegetables such as *aojiso* (beefsteak plant) and *shiitaké* (an edible fungus) are used as the ingredients for the *tempura.*

Sashimi

Sashimi is usually served as an accompaniment to *shōkadō-bentō.* Less expensive versions use cheaper ingredients such as *maguro* or *ika,* while more expensive versions use expensive, seasonal seafood such as *tai* (sea bream) or *kisu.*

Nimono

The *nimono* used in *shōkadō-bentō* usually consists of vegetables such as *hasu* (lotus root), *kinusaya* (young pea-pods), plus *kōyadōfu* (see p. 149), *yuba* (see p. 148) or other boiled delicacies. The *nimono* is flavoured with soy sauce, sugar, *mirin* (sweet *saké*) and *saké* (see p.140).

Yakimono

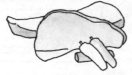

The *tempura* or *nimono* is sometimes replaced by *yakimono.* This often consists of *teriyaki,* a style of cooking in which *buri* (yellowtail), chicken or other ingredients are brushed with soy sauce and grilled.

Enkai-ryōri

宴会料理

The Japanese like to gather for food and drink parties whenever there is anything to celebrate. Such occasions include parties for company employees leaving or joining a place of work; weddings, and lesser occasions of all descriptions. The food served depends on the occasion, but these parties all have the same purpose; to deepen mutual understanding and friendship.

The number of people at a party depends on why it is being held, but it usually involves sitting down around tables rather than standing up as at Western-style cocktail parties. Each person is served a course of food, and everybody fills each other's glasses as a sign of friendship.

Yaki-zakana
(grilled fish)

Yasai-no-nimono
(stewed vegetables)

Sashimi (raw fish)

The most elaborate parties in Japan are wedding receptions. The food served on these occasions can amount to a sumptuous banquet, with especially auspicious dishes such as *isé-ebi* (lobster) and whole grilled *tai* (sea bream) taking pride of place.

The food served at *enkai* (parties) depends on the budget, but is usually typical Japanese food as described in this book — something grilled, such as a whole fish; something fried, such as *tempura*; something raw, such as *sashimi*; something steamed, such as *chawan-mushi*, something stewed, such as vegetables; a rice dish, such as *sushi*; etc.

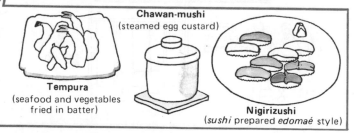

Chawan-mushi
(steamed egg custard)

Tempura
(seafood and vegetables fried in batter)

Nigirizushi
(*sushi* prepared *edomaé* style)

Gatherings at which food and drink are served are held mournful as well as happy occasions. A typical example is the *hōji*, a Buddhist memorial service held in memory of loved ones who have passed away. After the service, all those attending gather for a meal together.

Kanji (organizer)

When people hold a party such as *bōnenkai* (literally, "forget-the-year-parties") or *shinnenkai* (New Year parties), they usually choose an organizer called a *kanji*. The *kanji* is responsible for reserving the place where the party will be held, collecting the money and paying the bill, and making sure everything goes smoothly during the actual event.

Miso-shiru みそ汁

Miso-shiru (*miso* soup) is almost always served when the meal includes a bowl of rice. The taste varies from restaurant to restaurant and family to family, depending on what the stock is made from and what variety of *miso* (see p.158) is used.

1) Heat a piece of *kombu* (kelp) in water until boiling. Remove the *kombu*. Add *katsuo-bushi* (dried bonito shavings) and boil.

2) Pour the stock through a strainer to remove the *katsuo-bushi*.

Kai (shellfish)

Nasu (eggplant)

Wakamé (a type of seaweed)

Tōfu (bean curd)

Jaga-imo (potato)

3) Add the ingredients to the stock and boil until cooked. Dissolve the *miso* in a little of the stock and add it to the pot; heat, but do not boil.

Suimono 吸い物

It is a clear soup made without *miso*, containing fairly expensive ingredients such as prawn, chicken or clam. The *dashi* (stock) on which it is based is usually of higher quality than that used for *miso-shiru*.

Salt

Soy sauce

Stock

The ingredients are cooked separately and placed in the soup bowls, and the soup is then poured on top.

Suimono is seasoned lightly with soy sauce and salt.

Suikuchi

Mitsuba
(trefoil)

Yuzu
(Chinese lemon)

Negi
(spring onions)

Goma
(sesame)

Nori
(dried seaweed)

Various ingredients such as *mitsuba* (trefoil), *yuzu* (Chinese lemon), *shōga* (ginger), *goma* (sesame), *nori* (dried seaweed) and *negi* (spring onions) are used to give *suimono* an appetizing aroma. This aroma is known as *suikuchi*.

RICE DISHES
&
PICKLES

Rice is the staple food
for Japanese people. This
white, tasteless (has subtle flavor)
rice is cooked in such various ways
as fried, mixed with vegetables
and meats or covered with a
sauce. Each dish has a
different flavor.

Katsu-don
カツ丼

A *domburi* is a porcelain bowl with a lid, and *domburimono* is the general term for rice dishes served in this type of bowl. The bowl is filled about two-thirds full with boiled rice, and toppings such as beef, chicken, egg, *tempura,* etc., are placed on top. Almost all *soba-ya, udon-ya* and popular restaurants serve *domburimono.*

The *tonkatsu* (see p.43) is boiled together with sliced onions in a broth made from stock, soy sauce, sugar, and *saké.* An egg is then broken over the top of the *tonkatsu,* which is then served on top of rice in a *domburi.* This dish is called *katsu-don* and is the most popular type of *domburimono.*

Tamanegi (onions)

Egg

Sliced *tonkatsu*

Katsu-don usually comes with *miso-shiru (miso* soup) and a few slices of *tsukemono* (pickles).

Ten-don
天丼

Ten-don is a *domburi* dish in which freshly-fried *tempura* is placed on top of rice in a china bowl and covered with *tentsuyu* (a hot broth). This dish is available at most *tempura-ya* (*tempura* restaurants), *soba-ya* (*soba* restaurants) and *shokudō* (restaurants and dining-halls). The *tempura* most often used for this dish is *ebi* (prawn).

Ten-don

Tenjū

Tenjū is similar to *tendon* except that it is usually served in a lacquer box, and rather more expensive *tempura* is used.

--- **Domburi pan and Domburimono sauce** ---

The special *nabé*, or pan, used for cooking *domburimono* holds just the right amount of ingredients to put on top of the rice in the *domburi*.

This sauce, made from stock, soy sauce, sugar, *mirin* (sweet *saké*) and other ingredients, is used with almost every form of *domburimono*.

Mirin (sweet *saké*)　Salt　Soy sauce

Oyako-don & Tamago-don

親子丼・玉子丼

The name of *oyako-don* means "parent-and-child *domburi*". The "parent" is chicken and the "child" is egg. The dish is prepared by boiling chicken and onions in *domburi* sauce, adding a beaten egg and cooking until the egg sets, and pouring it all onto rice in a china bowl. *Tamago-don* is *oyako-don* without the chicken.

Sliced onions

Chicken

Beaten egg

Mitsuba (trefoil)

Mitsuba is often used as a flavoring in *domburimono*.

Demaé

Demaé is a very handy service provided by restaurants. With just one telephone call, you can have a hot meal delivered speedily to your door. Local *soba-ya* (*soba* restaurants), *sushi-ya* (*sushi* restaurants) and *rāmen-ya* (*rāmen* restaurants) all offer this service, and most have a special *demaé* menu. The meals are usually delivered on motor bikes equipped with special non-spill carriers on the back.

Chūka-don & *Tenshin-don*
中華丼・天津丼

Chūka-don is a *domburi* dish consisting of *happōsai* (bamboo shoots, pieces of pork, vegetables, etc., in a thick, clear sauce) on top of rice. *Tenshin-don* is egg omelette containing pieces of crab, again served on top of rice. Both these dishes, originally Chinese dishes, are available at Chinese restaurants and *shokudō* (general restaurants and dining-halls).

Chūka-don

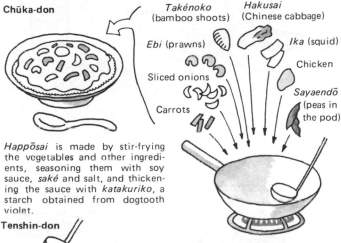

Takénoko (bamboo shoots)

Hakusai (Chinese cabbage)

Ebi (prawns)

Ika (squid)

Sliced onions

Chicken

Carrots

Sayaendō (peas in the pod)

Happōsai is made by stir-frying the vegetables and other ingredients, seasoning them with soy sauce, *saké* and salt, and thickening the sauce with *katakuriko*, a starch obtained from dogtooth violet.

Tenshin-don

Cook a mixture of egg and pieces of crab in a round pan and place the resulting omelette on top of rice. Before serving, pour a thick sauce made from soy sauce, salt, stock, and *katakuriko,* over the top.

Curry was first introduced into Japan toward the 19th century, and it rapidly became adapted to the Japanese taste. The dish known as *karē-raisu* (curry and rice) consists of meat and vegetables in a sweetish, curry-flavored sauce, on top of rice, and is served at all kinds of popular restaurants as well as in homes.

Karē-raisu

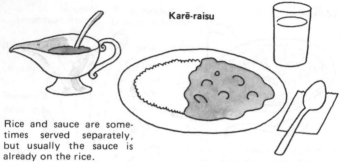

Rice and sauce are sometimes served separately, but usually the sauce is already on the rice.

Shiba-zuké
(see p.88)

Fukujin-zuké

Rakkyō-zuké
(pickled shallots)

Karē-udon

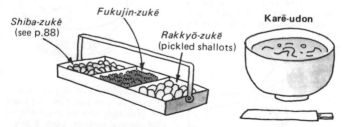

Karē-raisu is invariably accompanied by the red pickles known as *fukujin-zuké* (see p. 87).

This dish consists of *udon* (wheat noodles) in a curry-flavored soup.

Hayashi-raisu
ハヤシライス

This dish is an adaptation of the Western dish hashed beef. It consists of thinly-sliced beef and onions fried in butter, flavored with tomato ketchup, soy sauce and other seasonings, and served on top of rice. *Hayashi-raisu* is an excellent example of a Western dish adapted to the Japanese taste.

HOW TO PREPARE HAYASHI-RAISU

Hayashi-sauce

Rice

4) Serve the rice with *hayashi*-sauce on top of it.

1) Slice beef, onions and carrots thinly.

flour

2) Fry the ingredients lightly in butter. Add flour and thicken.

Tomato ketchup

Worcester sauce

3) Boil the ingredients in stock flavored with tomato ketchup, worcester sauce, soy sauce, etc.

Omu-raisu & *Chikin-raisu*
オムライス・チキンライス

Omu-raisu consists of rice mixed with pieces of chicken and flavored with tomato ketchup or purée, wrapped in a thin egg omelette case. It is usually decorated with a dab or two of ketchup on the top.

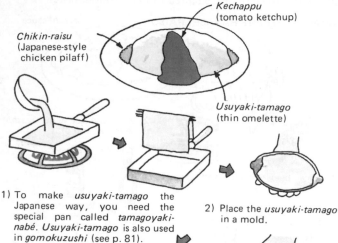

Kechappu (tomato ketchup)

Chikin-raisu (Japanese-style chicken pilaff)

Usuyaki-tamago (thin omelette)

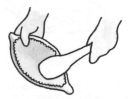

1) To make *usuyaki-tamago* the Japanese way, you need the special pan called *tamagoyaki-nabé*. *Usuyaki-tamago* is also used in *gomokuzushi* (see p. 81).

2) Place the *usuyaki-tamago* in a mold.

3) Fill the mold with *chikin-raisu*.

4) Turn the contents out onto a plate and decorate the top with tomato ketchup.

Chāhan & Okosama-ranchi
チャーハン・お子様ランチ

Chāhan (mixed fried rice) was originally a Chinese dish but has now become standard fare in Japan and is a popular way of using up left-over rice at home. *Okosama-ranchi* is a set meal for children, with small portions of everything from soup to dessert on the same plate.

Chāhan

Chāhan consists of fried rice mixed with small pieces of grilled pork, egg, *negi* (spring onions) and peas. It is usually served with a small bowl of clear soup.

Okosama-ranchi

Ice cream

Salad

French fried potatoes

Fried chicken

Fried prawns

Gratin

Chikin-raisu
(Japanese-style chicken pilaff)

Each restaurant prepares its own version of *okosama-ranchi*, but this meal is always arranged to appeal to children and is reasonably-priced. The dish on which it is served often takes the form of a car, boat, train, etc.

Onigiri
おにぎり

Onigiri (rice balls) are a handy, portable food equivalent to the Western sandwich. They are designed to keep for a fairly long time, since both the rice and the fillings used are seasoned with salt. Fillings used include *uméboshi* (see p. 86), *shiojaké*, and *tarako*, and the *onigiri* are usually wrapped in a sheet of *nori* (dried seaweed).

HOW TO MAKE ONIGIRI

Place the filling on top of some rice and cover with more rice. Squeeze the rice into a ball in both hands and sprinkle the ball with salt.

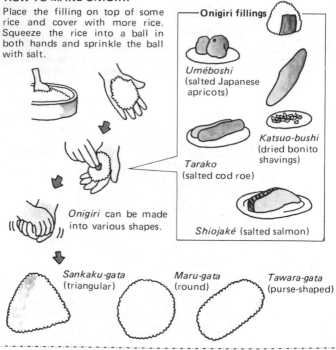

Onigiri can be made into various shapes.

Onigiri fillings

Uméboshi (salted Japanese apricots)

Katsuo-bushi (dried bonito shavings)

Tarako (salted cod roe)

Shiojaké (salted salmon)

Sankaku-gata (triangular)

Maru-gata (round)

Tawara-gata (purse-shaped)

Gomokuzushi is one of the types of *sushi* most commonly made at home. It consists of *sushi* rice with various vegetables boiled in soy sauce and sugar and arranged on the top and covered in strips of *usuyaki-tamago* (thin plain omelette). The topping ingredients are arranged to give an attractive combination of colors.

Inarizushi consists of small bags of *abura-age* (fried *tōfu*) boiled in soy sauce and sugar and filled with rice. It is made into various shapes.

Inarizushi

Tawara-gata

Sankaku-gata (triangular)

**┌HOW TO MAKE SUSHI-MESHI┐
   (SUSHI RICE)**

To make *sushi-meshi* (also known as *shari*), season freshly-cooked rice with a mixture of vinegar, sugar and salt.

Gomokuzushi

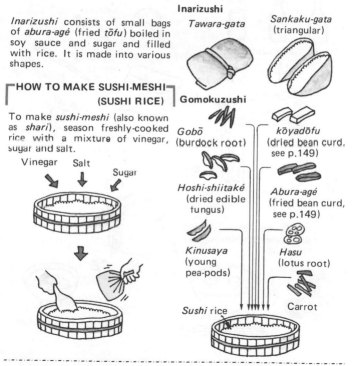

Vinegar Salt Sugar

Gobō (burdock root)

kōyadōfu (dried bean curd, see p.149)

Hoshi-shiitaké (dried edible tungus)

Abura-agé (fried bean curd, see p.149)

Kinusaya (young pea-pods)

Hasu (lotus root)

Sushi rice

Carrot

Kayaku-gohan
かやくごはん

Kayaku-gohan, also called *gomoku-gohan*, consists of boiled rice seasoned with soy sauce and mixed with a variety of different ingredients. The seasoning makes the rice a light brown color. Ingredients mixed with the rice include *shimeji* (an edible fungus), *satsuma-imo* (sweet potato) and many others.

Salt

Saké Soy sauce

Carrots

Shiitaké (edible fungus)

Gobō (burdock root)

Hijiki (brown algae)

Chicken

Abura-agé (fried *tōfu*)

Kuri-gohan

Kuri-gohan is boiled rice mixed with *kuri* (sweet chestnuts) and seasoned with salt.

Kayaku-gohan

Sekihan & Okowa
赤飯・おこわ

Sekihan (red rice) is served at birthdays, weddings, and other occasions of celebration. It is made with *mochigomé* (glutinous rice) mixed with *sasagé* (black-eyed peas) and steamed in the special steaming basket called *seiro*. The color of the *sasagé* turns the rice pink.

Mochigomé (glutinous rice)

Sasagé (black-eyed peas)

Seiro

Gomashio (salt and sesame)

A *seiro* is a bamboo basket used for steaming. It is placed on top of a pot containing boiling water.

Gomashio consists of black sesame seeds mixed with toasted salt. It is sprinkled on the top of *sekihan* before serving.

Sansai-okowa

Kinoko (mushroom)

Zemmai (flowering fern)

Okowa, which also means "hard", is steamed *mochigomé* (glutinous rice). It is mixed with *sansai* (mountain vegetables, see p. 100) to make *sansai-okowa*, with sweet chestnuts to make *kuri-okowa*, and with various other ingredients.

Warabi (bracken)

Takenoko (bamboo shoots)

Chazuké is rice in a bowl with green tea or fish stock poured over the top. It is garnished with various kinds of fish and vegetables and is drunk straight from the bowl. It is a handy way of using up left-over rice at home, and is also on the menus of many *yakitori-ya* and other drinking and eating establishments.

Green tea

Season *dashi-jiru* (stock) with soy sauce, salt and *saké*. Pour this over the rice.

TYPES OF CHAZUKÉ

Saké-chazuké
(*chazuké* with salted salmon)

Tarako-chazuké
(*chazuké* with salted cod roe)

Tai-chazuké
(*chazuké* with sea bream)

Nori-chazuké
(*chazuké* with dried seaweed)

Okayu & Zōsui
おかゆ・雑炊

Okayu (rice gruel) is rice cooked until it is very soft and watery. It is seasoned with salt and mixed with egg or other ingredients and is often given to invalids, since it is easily eaten and digested. It is usually eaten with *umeboshi* (salted Japanese apricots). *Zōsui* is rice soup containing crab, vegetables, or other ingredients.

MAKING OKAYU

Put the rice with more than five parts water in a thick earthenware or metal pot, season with salt, and cook slowly for a long time.

Umeboshi

MAKING ZŌSUI

Cook the rice in a soup made from stock seasoned with soy sauce and salt, and add vegetables, egg, fish or other ingredients to taste.

Salt   Soy sauce   Stock

Egg
Shiitaké (edible fungus)   Chicken
Carrots   *Daikon* (Japanese radish)

Rice

Tsukemono

漬物

Tsukemono (pickles) developed as a way of preserving vegetables. The method of pickling and the vegetables themselves vary from region to region, but no Japanese meal is complete without them. Methods of pickling include *shio-zuké* (salting), *su-zuké* (pickling in vinegar) and *shōyu-zuké* (preserving in soy sauce), etc.

Takuan-zuké

Takuan, or pickled *daikon* (Japanese radish) is prepared by burying whole *aki-daikon* (autumn radishes) in tubs full of salted *nuka* (rice bran).

Umeboshi

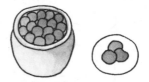

One of the best-known of pickles is the *umeboshi*, or salted Japanese apricot. This consists of *umé* packed in salt and colored red with *akajiso* (red beefsteak plant) leaves.

HOW TO MAKE UMEBOSHI

1) Wash *umé* well, and mix salt with it.

2) Knead *akajiso* in salt, place *umé* and *shiso* into a pickle crock.

3) Put a weight on the them.

4) Leave them to mature for 3 to 4 weeks, then drain all the water. Sun dry *umé* and *akajiso* leaves for a few days.

Hakusai-zuké

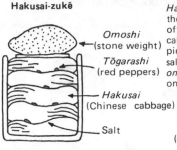

Omoshi
(stone weight)

Tōgarashi
(red peppers)

Hakusai
(Chinese cabbage)

Salt

Hakusai (Chinese cabbages) are at their best in winter, and they are often preserved by salting. Each cabbage is cut into four or eight pieces and packed with layers of salt and *tōgarashi* in a tub. An *omoshi* (stone weight) is then put on the top.

Nuka-zuké

Nasu
(eggplant)

Kabu
(turnip)

Kyūri
(cucumber)

Nuka, or rice bran, is the husks left behind when rice is polished. It is mixed with salt, water and spices to form the thick paste called *nukadoko* ("bed of *nuka*") in which vegetables to be preserved are buried. This method of pickling is quicker than others, and vegetables preserved in this way can usually be eaten within a day or so.

Kasu-zuké

In this method of pickling, vegetables are buried in a paste made from *shōchū* (see p. 142), sugar and *sakékasu*, the lees from the *saké*-making process.

Japanese Tsukemono (Pickles)

There are many other pickles dear to the Japanese heart (and stomach). These include salted *nasu* (eggplant) and *kyūri* (cucumber), and the red pickled *daikon* and cucumber called *fukujin-zuké* that is always served with *karē-raisu* (see p. 76).

HOW TO MAKE RAKKYŌ-ZUKÉ (PICKLED SHALLOTS)

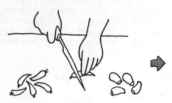

1) Wash the *rakkyō* and top and tail them.

2) Pack them in salt with a weight on the top.

3) Pour off the water and pack the salted *rakkyō* in a bottle. Cover with vinegar boiled with sugar and *aka-tōgarashi* (red peppers).

Vinegar Sugar Red peppers

Nishin-zuké

This is a specialty of Hokkaidō, with its cold climate. Dried *nishin* (herring) is pickled with *daikon* (Japanese radish) and cabbage in *kōji* (malted rice) and salt.

Shiba-zuké

Kyōto's most famous pickle, *shiba-zuké*, consists of *kyūri, nasu, myōga* (Japanese ginger), *ao-tōgarashi* (green peppers), *shiso* (beefsteak plant) and other local vegetables preserved in salt.

NOODLE DISHES

Japanese people
often eat not only rice
dishes but also noodle
especially 'soba', 'udon' and
'rāmen' which are inexpensive.
You can enjoy a wide variety of
noodle dishes by changing the
combination of soup and ingredients. Noodle dishes
reflect the sense of
taste of the general
Japanese people.

Soba & Udon
そば・うどん

Soba are thin brownish noodles made from a mixture of *soba-ko* (buckwheat flour) and wheat flour. *Udon,* which is made from wheat flour only, is a similar color to spaghetti but is softer. Some *soba* dishes, such as *mori-soba,* are served cold, with a side dish of soy-based broth into which the *soba* is dipped before being eaten. Other *soba* dishes and most *udon* dishes consist of a bowl of the noodles in hot broth, together with various other ingredients such as vegetables, eggs, *abura-agē,* or meat. The broth is made from soy sauce, *mirin* (sweet *sakē*), sugar, and stock.

Mori-soba

Yakumi (chopped *negi, wasabi*)

Waribashi

Mori-soba is the most popular form of cold *soba*. The *soba* is served on a bamboo rack in a lacquer box, with a small bowl of broth and a small dish of chopped *negi* (spring onions) and *wasabi* (Japanese horseradish). The condiments should be mixed into the broth and the noodles dipped into the mixture before eating.

Tokkuri (flask) containing *taré* (soy-based broth)

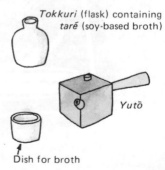

A *yutō* is a wooden, often square, lacquered container. Some of the hot broth in which the *soba* was boiled is placed in it and served to customers who have eaten *mori-soba* or *zaru-soba.* This broth, called *sobayu,* should be mixed with the remaining broth into which the *soba* was dipped, and drunk.

Yutō

Dish for broth

Zaru-soba is exactly the same as mori-soba except that it is covered with thin strips of *nori* (dried seaweed), making it slightly more expensive.

Zaru-soba

Kitsunē

Kitsunē is the most popular form of hot *soba* or *udon.* It consists of the noodles in hot broth with *negi* (spring onions) and *abura-agé* (fried *tōfu*) (see p.149) on top.

Tanuki

Tanuki is similar to *Kitsunē* but with *agedama* (fried *tempura* batter) instead of *abura-agé.* The *agedama* gives the hot noodle broth richness and flavour.

How to Order

Most *soba-ya* serve both *soba* and *udon,* so it is necessary to specify which you want when ordering. To order the *kitsunē* style, for example, you must ask for either "*kitsunē-soba*" or "*kitsunē-udon*". Note that *mori-soba* and *zaru-soba* come in the *soba* form only. Similarly, *nabeyaki-udon* (a winter dish of *udon* with vegetables, *tempura,* egg, etc., served in a casserole with a lid) comes in the *udon* form only.

Okamé

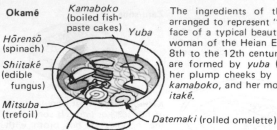

Kamaboko (boiled fish-paste cakes)
Yuba
Hōrensō (spinach)
Shiitaké (edible fungus)
Mitsuba (trefoil)
Datemaki (rolled omelette)
Naruto (slices of boiled fish paste with a pink swirl in the center)

The ingredients of this dish are arranged to represent "*okamé*", the face of a typical beautiful Japanese woman of the Heian Era (from the 8th to the 12th century). Her eyes are formed by *yuba* (see p. 148), her plump cheeks by two slices of *kamaboko*, and her mouth by a *shiitaké*.

This *soba* or *udon* dish gets its name from the raw egg broken over the top of the noodles in their hot broth. The egg looks like a full moon, and "*tsukimi*" is the custom of viewing the full moon at harvest time.

Tsukimi

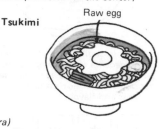

Raw egg

Tempura

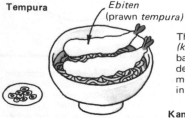

Ebiten (prawn *tempura*)

The highlight of this dish is *ebiten* (*kuruma ebi*, or prawn, coated in batter made from wheat flour and deep-fried). This is usually the most expensive dish to be found in a *soba-ya* (*soba* restaurant).

Kamo-namban

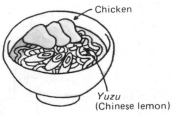

Chicken

Yuzu (Chinese lemon)

Kamo means duck, and this dish originally consisted of soft duck meat sliced thinly and boiled in *soba* broth, together with toasted *negi*, on top of *soba* or *udon*. However, chicken is usually used instead of duck nowadays.

Nabeyaki-udon

Fu (wheat gluten cake)

Hōrensō (spinach)

Egg

Donabé (earthenware pot with lid)

Kamaboko (cake made from boiled fish paste)

Nabeyaki is eaten mainly in winter. *Udon* is placed together with the other ingredients and the stock in a *donabé,* and boiled. The dish is served piping hot in the *nabé* in which it is cooked.

Kama-agé-udon

Kama-agé consists of hot *udon* served in a wooden tub and dipped into hot broth before eating. The condiments to be mixed into the broth include *kezuribushi* (flakes of dried bonito), *negi* (spring onions), and *shōga* (ginger).

Toshikoshi-soba

It is an ancient tradition on New Year's Eve in Japan to eat *soba* while listening to the temple bells ringing in the New Year. *Soba* eaten on this occasion is called *toshikoshi-soba,* and the long, thin noodles represent a wish for long life.

93

Yakumi

Yakumi is the name given to the condiments used to enhance the plain taste of *soba* and *udon.* Some are designed to impart an appetizing aroma and some to draw out the flavour.

Negi

The most common form of condiment is *negi* (spring onions), which are liked for their sharp, clean taste and smell. They are used with both hot and cold *soba.*

Shichimi

Shichimi, which literally means "seven tastes", is a blend of *mikan* (mandarin orange) peel, *sanshō* (Japanese pepper), *kurogoma* (black sesame), *asanomi* (hemp-seeds), *keshi* (poppy seeds), *tō-garashi* (cayenne pepper) and *hoshinori* (dried *nori,* or edible seaweed). It is used with hot *soba* and *udon.*

Wasabi

Wasabi, or Japanese horseradish, is a pungent, pale-green condiment made by grating the *wasabi* root. It is always served with *mori* and *zaru-soba.*

Mitsuba

The *mitsuba,* or trefoil, brings a taste of spring to the dishes it seasons. Its leaves are greeny-yellow.

Yuzu

The *yuzu,* or Chinese lemon, has a unique fragrance subtly different from that of other citrus fruit. The peel is used to flavour various dishes in winter.

Hiyamugi & Sōmen
冷麦・そうめん

Hiyamugi and *sōmen* are like *udon* but thinner; *hiyamugi* is about 1.5 mm.in diameter and *sōmen* about 1.0 mm. The dried noodles are boiled in hot water, rinsed in cold water, and eaten cold after being dipped in cold broth. They are very popular in summer.

This is eaten by dipping the noodles and other ingredients into broth mixed with various condiments.

Hiyamugi

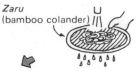

Mikan
(Mandarin orange)

Cherry

Shiso
(beefsteak plant leaf)

Sōmen

This is eaten in the same way as *hiya-mugi*. In some districts, the *sōmen* is washed down a long pipe made of split bamboo, and the diners scoop the noodles out of the flowing water with their chop sticks.

HOW TO COOK HIYAMUGI AND SŌMEN

2) Place the noodles in a *zaru* and rinse them thoroughly in cold water.

Zaru
(bamboo colander)

1) Boil *hiyamugi* for five to six minutes, *sōmen* for two to three minutes.

Ice

3) Drain the noodles and place them in a serving dish with ice cubes.

Rāmen, or Chinese noodles, are yellowish in color and are made from wheat flour, egg, salt, and *kansui,* a kind of mineral water. They are boiled and served in a hot soup made from pork or chicken bones. The soup is seasoned with *shōyu* (soy sauce), *miso* (fermented soy-bean paste) or *shio* (salt), and a variety of other ingredients such as *chāshū, memma, naruto* and *negi* are added.

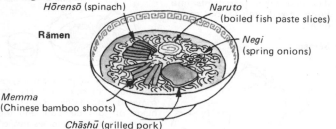

Rāmen

Hōrensō (spinach)

Naruto (boiled fish paste slices)

Negi (spring onions)

Memma (Chinese bamboo shoots)

Chāshū (grilled pork)

Chāshūmen

This is a variety of *rāmen* with slices of *chāshū* (grilled pork) on the top. The pork is brushed with soy sauce before being grilled.

Batā-rāmen

This is simply *miso-rāmen* (*rāmen* in *miso*-flavored soup) with a knob of butter.

Hiyashi-chūka

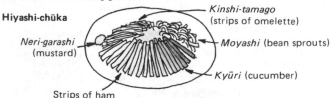

Kinshi-tamago (strips of omelette)

Neri-garashi (mustard)

Moyashi (bean sprouts)

Kyūri (cucumber)

Strips of ham

Hiyashi-chūka consists of cold, boiled Chinese noodles served with thin strips of ham, vegetables, etc. It is served in a sweet, vinegary sauce made from soy sauce, vinegar, sugar, and *goma* (sesame).

Mistakenly called *soba*, *yaki-soba* is actually steamed Chinese noodles mixed with stir-fried vegetables and pieces of meat. There are two kinds of *yaki-soba* – the soft kind is made by frying the noodles together with the other ingredients and seasoned with sauce, and the hard kind (*kata-yaki-soba*) is made by deep-frying the noodles alone and then adding the other ingredients together with a thick sauce.

Yaki-soba

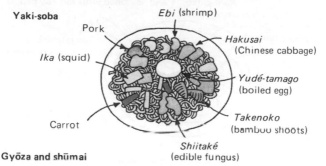

Pork

Ebi (shrimp)

Ika (squid)

Hakusai (Chinese cabbage)

Yudé-tamago (boiled egg)

Carrot

Takenoko (bamboo shoots)

Shiitaké (edible fungus)

Gyōza and shūmai

Gyōza and *shūmai* are often eaten as an accompaniment to *rāmen* or *yaki-soba* when the latter are not filling enough. They both consist of Chinese pastry cases made from wheat flour and stuffed with vegetables and ground meat. *Gyōza* are fried in oil, while *shūmai* are steamed.

Gyōza

Shūmai

Soy sauce

Su (vinegar)

Rāyu (a hot oil made from sesame oil and cayenne pepper)

Nerigarashi (Mustard)

Champon & Sara-udon
チャンポン・皿うどん

Champon and *sara-udon* are noodle dishes which originated in Nagasaki, in Kyūshū. They both consist of Chinese noodles with plenty of vegetables, fish, and meat.

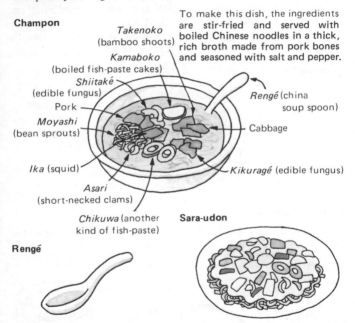

Champon

To make this dish, the ingredients are stir-fried and served with boiled Chinese noodles in a thick, rich broth made from pork bones and seasoned with salt and pepper.

Takenoko (bamboo shoots)

Kamaboko (boiled fish-paste cakes)

Shiitaké (edible fungus)

Pork

Moyashi (bean sprouts)

Ika (squid)

Asari (short-necked clams)

Chikuwa (another kind of fish-paste)

Rengé (china soup spoon)

Cabbage

Kikuragé (edible fungus)

Rengé

Sara-udon

The *rengé*, a large china soup spoon, is always supplied with hot Chinese noodle dishes and *nabemono* (see p.31).

Sara-udon is very similar to hard *yaki-soba* (see p.97). The same ingredients as used in *champon* are coated in thick sauce and placed on top of Chinese noodles.

SEASONAL
&
REGIONAL
COOKING

The Japanese people
have a basic concept toward
food as being simple to cook, seasonal and locally grown. In this
way they are able to enjoy the
passing of the four seasons.

Haru-no-aji

春の味 (Seasonal Cooking in Spring)

Spring is the time when plants are in bud, and many bitter-tasting vegetables are on the market. Such vegetables are boiled or fried in oil to remove the bitterness and seasoned with sweet seasonings. Spring is also the best time for shellfish.

Takenoko

Takenoko (bamboo shoots) are dug up when they poke their heads above the ground in May. They are boiled in big pots and used in a variety of dishes, such as *tosani* (*takenoko* boiled in soy sauce and covered liberally with *katsuo-bushi* (dried bonito shavings)), ***takenoko-gohan*** (rice mixed with *takenoko*), etc.

Sansai

Literally "mountain vegetables", *sansai* are found in abundance in the hills and beside the ricefields in spring. They are usually boiled to remove their bitterness before being used in cooking. They are eaten cold with soy sauce and *katsuo-bushi* as *ohitashi,* or with *karashi* (mustard) and soy sauce as *karashi-aé;* or they are stir-fried and then boiled with soy sauce and sugar.

| *Warabi* (bracken) | *Zemmai* (flowering fern) | *Fuki* (bog rhubarb) | *Seri* (dropwort) |

Tai

Both its taste and its appearance make the *tai* (sea bream) an aristocrat of fish. The pink *sakura-dai* is usually salted and grilled whole for wedding banquets and other celebrations, or eaten raw as *sashimi*; and a salty soup called *ushio-jiru* is made with the head. The light, sweetish taste of *tai* is truly delicious.

Sawara

The soft, white flesh of the *sawara* (Spanish mackerel) is used in the form of fillets. It is salted and grilled as *shio-yaki*, or marinated in soy sauce, *saké*, *mirin* (sweet *saké*) and *yuzu* (Chinese lemon) and then grilled, as *yūan-yaki*.

Hamaguri

Hamaguri (clams) are a vital part of **momo-no-sekku** (*hina-matsuri*, the Doll's Festival, in March). They are cooked in their shells, as *yaki-hamaguri*, or used together with *mitsuba* (trefoil) as an ingredient of *sumashi-jiru* (clear soup).

Asari

Asari (short necked clams) are at their best from February to April. *Asari* are boiled in their shells as an ingredient of *miso-shiru* (*miso* soup), or removed from their shells and boiled in soy sauce and sugar to make *tsukudani*.

--- **Sunadashi** ---

Salt

Since shellfishes such as *hamaguri* and *asari* bury themselves in the sand, they must be thoroughly cleaned before being used in cooking. They will eject the sand by themselves if left for half a day in water containing 1 or 2% of salt.

101

Natsu-no-aji

夏の味 (Seasonal Cooking in Summer)

Summer in most parts of Japan is unpleasantly hot and humid, and most summer cooking uses salt and vinegar to give a light, refreshing taste and stimulate jaded appetites.

Soramamé and Edamamé

Beer becomes even more popular than usual in summer, and boiled and salted *soramamé* (broad beans) and *edamamé* (green soybeans) are two of the most popular *tsumami* (drink snacks) to nibble while drinking.

Nasu

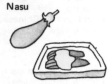

The best-known dish using *nasu* is *shigi-yaki*, which consists of halved *nasu* grilled and covered in *neri-miso* (*miso* sweetened and spiced with sugar, *saké* and ginger).

Umé

June is the *umé* (Japanese apricot) season. These are hard and green and cannot be eaten as they are. The green ones are used for *umeshu* (an *umé*-flavored alcoholic drink), and the slightly riper, yellowish ones for *uméboshi* (salted *umé*, see p. 86).

Maguro

The *maguro* (tuna) is a highly popular fish eaten mainly in the form of *sashimi* or *sushi*. Another well-liked *maguro* dish is *yamakaké*, which consists of raw *maguro* cut into bite-sized chunks and covered in grated *yamaimo* (yam) and *nori* (dried seaweed).

Toro

Chū-toro

Ō-toro

Different parts of the *maguro* have different names and different tastes. The most sought-after part is the belly, called *toro*, which is light pink and has a high oil content.

Katsuo

The most popular form of *sashimi* in summer is *katsuo-no-tataki*, raw *katsuo* (bonito) lightly seasoned with vinegar. Since it is already seasoned, *katsuo-no-tataki* is not dipped in soy sauce like other *sashimi*.

PREPARING KATSUO-NO-TATAKI

1) Gut the fish, remove the head, and cut into five fillets.

2) Pierce with metal skewers and pass quickly over a flame to brown the skin.

3) Dip briefly in iced water, remove and wipe dry.

4) Cut into about 1-cm thick slices.

Vinegar   Soy sauce

5) For the garnish, grate *daikon* (Japanese radish), *ninniku* (garlic), and *shōga* (ginger), and chop *negi* (spring onions) finely. Prepare a sauce by mixing *su* (rice vinegar) and soy sauce.

6) Place the fish with the garnishes and sauce in a tray and beat the flavors in with the flat of a knife.

Ayu

The *ayu* (sweetfish) caught in June, called *waka-ayu* (young sweetfish), has soft skin and bones, but the ones caught at the end of July are slightly oilier and therefore taste better. They are salted and grilled and eaten with *tadezu*, vinegar mixed with the pungent crushed leaves of the *tadé* (smartweed).

Autumn in Japan is poetically called *"minori-no-aki"* (autumn — season of fruitfulness), since it is the season of harvests when plants lose their bitterness and become sweet and succulent, and fish are at their oil-rich best. Autumn dishes thus try simply to preserve the natural flavors and fragrances of the raw materials.

Matsutaké

The *matsutaké* is a highly-prized (and highly-priced) mushroom that features in many autumn dishes. Its scent and flavor are best just before the cap opens out. One of the best ways to appreciate the superb taste of the *matsutaké* is in the dish known as *hōroku-yaki*, in which the *matsutaké* is cooked on a hot stone inside a shallow earthenware pot with the lid on.

Kuri

Kuri (chestnuts) are steamed or boiled and eaten by themselves, or are steamed with rice and red beans to make the dish known as *kuri-okowa* (see p. 83). They are also used in making *wagashi* (Japanese-style cakes and sweets), and *kinton* (see p. 61).

Ginnan

The *ginnan*, the nut of the *ichō-no-ki* (gingko tree) has a hard, off-white shell. The kernel is pale-green, and oval-shaped, and is covered in a thin, light-brown skin. It is boiled to remove the skin and is then used in dishes such as *chawan-mushi* (steamed egg custard, see p.172) and *yosé-nabé* (hotpot).

Satsuma-imo

The *satsuma-imo* (sweet potato), a popular autumn snack, is often steamed or baked and eaten plain. It is also sliced and used in *tempura*, or mashed and incorporated into various kinds of cakes and sweets.

Samma

The *samma*, or saury, is a sword-shaped fish. In autumn, the oil content of *samma* is as much as 20%, so the best way of cooking it is to salt it and grill it. It is then eaten hot with *daikon-oroshi* (grated Japanese radish) and soy sauce or lemon.

Saba

The *saba*, or mackerel, is a strong-smelling fish which easily loses its freshness. When eaten raw, it is first salted and then marinated in vinegar — this is called *shimé-saba*. It is also boiled with ginger and *miso* and served as *misoni*, or made into a soup called *senba-jiru* with *daikon* (Japanese radish) and the juice of *shōga* (ginger).

HOW TO PREPARE SHIMÉ-SABA

1) Cut the fish into three fillets.

2) Arrange the fillets on a flat dish, cover them with salt, and leave them for three to five hours.

3) Wipe off the excess salt and place the fillets in vinegar, until the surface of the fish turns white.

4) Skin and slice thinly. Eat with *karashi* (mustard) and soy sauce.

Aji

The *aji* (horse mackerel), which does not have a strong smell, makes very pleasant eating. It is eaten raw in the form of *sashimi* or *sushi*, or cooked in either Western or Japanese style, e.g., salted and grilled (*shio-yaki*), or fried in batter (*furai*).

=== **Checking a Fish for Freshness:** ===

1) Are the eyes clear?

2) Are the scales all intact?

3) Are the gills bright red?

4) Is the flesh firm and resilient?

Fuyu-no-aji

冬の味 (Seasonal Cooking in Winter)

Fish and vegetables generally have a sweeter taste in winter, and winter dishes are seasoned lightly to allow the natural sweetness of the ingredients to come to the fore. Winter is the most popular season for *nabemono*, warming dishes which are usually cooked at the table in a big earthenware pot from which everyone helps themselves.

Daikon

The *daikon* (Japanese radish) loses its summer pungency when winter comes, becoming softer and sweeter. It is still grated or shredded and used as a garnish for *sashimi* (raw fish), and it is also used in a typical winter dish, *furofuki-daikon*. This consists of *daikon* cut into rings, boiled, and covered in *neri-miso*, a thick, sweet *miso* sauce made from *miso*, sugar, *saké* and stock.

Daikon from different areas have different shapes and different names, and are used in different ways:

Sakurajima-daikon
(used in stews)

Hōryō-daikon
(used in stews)

Moriguchi-daikon
(pickled in *saké* lees
to make *kasu-zuké*)

Nerima-daikon
(pickled in salt to
make *takuan-zuké*)

Yuzu

The *yuzu*, or Chinese lemon, has the best bouquet of all the citrus-fruit family. The peel is cut thinly and used to flavor *nabemono* (hot-pots) and other dishes, or is grated and mixed with *miso* (fermented soy-bean paste) to make *yuzu-miso* for *dengaku* (see p.112) or *furofuki-daikon*.

Hakusai

The simple taste of *hakusai* (Chinese cabbage) means that this useful vegetable goes well with almost any dish. It is added to almost all *nabe-mono* (hotpot) and makes the most common form of *tsukemono* (pickles) when preserved in salt.

Ankō

Except for the head and the bones, every part of the *ankō* (or angler fish) can be eaten. The flesh and skin are used in *nabe-mono* (hotpots), called *ankō-nabé* (see p.34).

Fugu

The *fugu,* or swellfish, is also a winter fish. It is eaten as the *nabe-mono* (hotpot) called *chiri-nabé*, with *hakusai* (Chinese cabbage), *tōfu* (bean curd), etc.; and its fin is steeped in hot *saké* to make the warming drink called *hiré-zaké*. Only licensed *fugu* chefs are allowed to prepare this fish in Japan, since it contains a deadly poison.

Chiri-nabé

Kaki

Kaki (oysters)

Kombu (kelp)

Small portable cooker

Kaki (oysters) should be eaten raw or cooked simply to preserve their unique, delicate flavor. One method of cooking them is *matsu-maé-yaki,* in which the oysters are placed on a large sheet of **kombu** (kelp) and grilled on one of the small portable cookers.

When to Eat Kaki

The season for *kaki,* as in other countries, is from September to March, i.e., during any month with an ''r'' in it.

There is fish in plenty whatever the season in Hokkaidō, the northernmost of Japan's main islands, but it is particularly well-known for its *saké* (salmon) and *nishin* (herring). Hokkaidō's winters are extremely cold, with many of the roads blocked by snow. Its best-known dishes are *nabemono* (hotpots) and *tsukemono* (pickles) based on these two fish.

Ishikari-nabé

Ikura (salmon roe)   *Saké* (salmon)

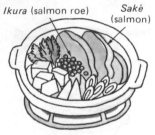

The River Ishikari, which flows through the center of Hokkaidō, is noted for the many salmon which return to it every year to spawn. *Ishikari-nabé* is a kind of hotpot based on *saké* (salmon) or *ikura* (salmon roe), with assorted vegetables. The stock is flavored with *miso* (see p.158).

Ruibé

Ruibé, which could be called "frozen *sashimi*", is made by freezing salmon or herring raw. It is served in thin slices while still slightly frozen.

Izushi

Izushi is a type of *sushi* made by placing slices of salmon, herring, *hatahata* (sandfish) or other fish on a mixture of rice and chopped carrot, and allowing the resulting dish to ferment. Although *sushi* is usually eaten as a main course, *izushi* is eaten as a side dish.

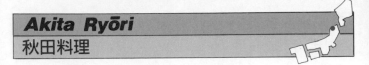

Akita, enclosed on three sides by mountains and on the fourth by the Sea of Japan, is famous for its clean water and its rice. This northerly region spends about three months of the year under snow, and its culinary specialty is *nabé-ryōri* (hotpots) using rice and fish.

Kiritampo-nabé

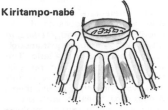

Kiritampo consists of boiled rice pounded into cakes and molded on sticks of *sugi* (Japanese cedar). The *Kiritampo* are lightly browned and then put in a *nabé* (hotpot) containing chicken, *negi* (spring onions), *gobō* (burdock root), and *satoimo* (taro) seasoned with soy sauce and *mirin* (sweet *saké*).

Shottsuru-nabé

In winter, Akita's fishermen make plentiful catches of *hata-hata* (sandfish). *Shottsuru* is a seasoning made by pickling *hata-hata* in salt, and *shottsuru-nabé* is a type of hotpot containing this seasoning.

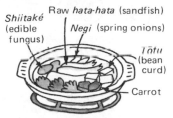

Shiitaké (edible fungus)
Raw *hata-hata* (sandfish)
Negi (spring onions)
Tōfu (bean curd)
Carrot

Jizaké

Where the rice is good, the *saké* is good too, and Akita pref. produces many local brands of excellent *kara-kuchi* (dry) *saké*.

Tomburi

Tomburi, which is dark brown and looks like caviare, is actually the seeds of the *hōkigusa*, or broom cypress. *Tomburi* is seasoned with soy sauce and eaten with yams cut into thin strips.

Iwaté & Miyagi Ryōri
岩手・宮城料理

Iwaté and Miyagi, which face the Pacific Ocean and the San-riku Sea, one of the world's three biggest fishing grounds, are famous for their *maguro* (tuna), *hoya* (sea squirt) and other seafood. They are also good producers of *soba* (buckwheat) and *mamé* (beans), which thrive in cold climates.

Wanko-soba (Iwaté)

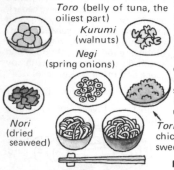

Toro (belly of tuna, the oiliest part)

Kurumi (walnuts)

Negi (spring onions)

Nori (dried seaweed)

Tori-soboro (minced chicken boiled in sweet, spicy sauce)

Iwaté Prefecture's specialty is *wanko-soba*. This consists of *soba* noodles in cold broth, served in tiny bowls containing just enough to be swallowed in one gulp. The waitress stands by and replaces the customers' bowls with full ones every time they empty them. *Wanko-soba* is eaten with six or seven different garnishes, making it a rather richer dish than the usual *soba*.

Harako-meshi (Miyagi)

Harako-meshi consists of boiled rice with *ikura* (salmon roe) on the top. The *ikura* are added just before the rice has finished cooking.

Hoya (Miyagi)

Hoya-no-sunomono

Hoya-no-misoyaki

Hoya (sea squirts) are at their best in early summer. One way of cooking them, called *hoya-no-misoyaki*, is to marinate them for one or two hours in a mixture of *miso*, *saké* and sugar, and then grill them. Another *hoya* dish is *hoya-no-sunomono*, *hoya* pickled in vinegar.

Tōkyō is the seat of Japan's government and culture and the center of its distribution network, and regional cooking from all over Japan is available in this great city. However, Tōkyō also has its own traditional cuisine, handed down from the days when it was known as Edo. This cuisine includes *nigirizushi*, *tempura* (see p. 36), and *tsukudani*.

Nigirizushi

Today, *sushi* is probably the best-known Japanese food. However, there are several different styles of *sushi* cuisine, and Tōkyō is famous for its *nigirizushi* (see p. 22). Another style of *sushi* is *oshizushi*, from the Kansai region, in which the rice, seafood and other ingredients are pressed in wooden molds and then cut into rectangular shapes.

Unagi-no kabayaki

Unagi (eel) is cooked *kabayaki* style by grilling it over charcoal while basting it with a thick soy-based sauce. In Tōkyō, the eel is filleted, boiled and then grilled, while in the Kansai region, it is grilled straight away without boiling.

Tsukudani

Tsukudani is a method of cooking in which the ingredients are boiled down for a long time in soy sauce. It has a strong taste and can only be eaten a little at a time. Ingredients used include small fish, *maguro* (tuna) cut into chunks, *kombu* (kelp), *asari* (short-necked clams), etc.

Kyōto Ryōri
京都料理

Most Kyōto cooking is done with fish brought in from other areas (since Kyōto has no coastline) and with local vegetables. Kyōto is the center for the refined cuisines known as *kaiseki-ryōri* (see p. 52) and *shōjin-ryōri* (see p. 56), and this is reflected in the everyday cooking of the area, with its artistic arrangement and seasonal variations.

Hamo-ryōri

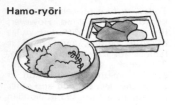

The *hamo* is a sea eel resembling the *unagi* (see p. 40). Two typical summer dishes in Kyōto are *otoshi*, which consists of *hamo* cut into small pieces and blanched in boiling water, and *hamo-yaki*, which is *hamo* basted with a sweet, spicy sauce and broiled over charcoal in the *kabayaki* style (see p. 40).

Sabazushi is a special kind of *oshi-zushi* consisting of salted and vinegared *saba* (mackerel) pressed on top of rice in box-shaped molds and cut into rectangles.

Sabazushi

Yudōfu

Dengaku

The good water of Kyōto is excellent for producing first-class *tōfu*. Two of the best-known dishes using *tōfu* are *yudōfu* (see p. 169) and *dengaku*, which consists of lightly-grilled *tōfu* with *kinomé-miso (miso* with *sanshō* — Japanese pepper — leaf buds) or *goma-miso* (sesame-flavored *miso*).

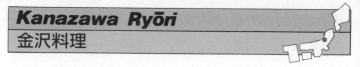

The local dishes of Kanazawa (Ishikawa pref.), on the Sea of Japan, are based mainly on the seafood taken from its rivers and marine fishing grounds.

Tai-no-karamushi

The dish is always served on occasions of celebration. It consists of *tai* (sea bream) stuffed with *ginnan* (gingko nuts), *asanomi* (hempseeds) assorted vegetables and *okara* (the lees from the *tōfu*-making process), and steamed. One *tai* serves several people.

Dojō (loaches, see p. 40) are a summer specialty. In Kanazawa, small *dojō* are skewered with the bones still in, seasoned with a sauce made from *mirin* (sweet *saké*) and soy sauce, and grilled over charcoal until crisp and crunchy.

Dojō-no-kabayaki

Iwana-no honezaké

In this rather refined method of drinking *saké*, the *iwana* (char), a fish which lives only in mountain streams, is grilled, and hot *saké* is then poured over it. The *saké* becomes imbued with the delicious flavor of the grilled fish.

Jibuni

Jibuni is a variation on chicken stew. Pieces of chicken are floured and stewed in a mixture of stock, soy sauce, sugar and *saké*, and vegetables and *kinoko* (mushroom) are added. When cooked, the stew is piled in a dish, covered in a thick sauce and decorated with *wasabi* (Japanese horseradish).

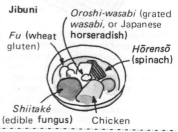

Oroshi-wasabi (grated *wasabi*, or Japanese horseradish)

Fu (wheat gluten)

Hōrensō (spinach)

Shiitaké (edible fungus)

Chicken

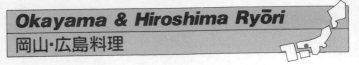

Okayama & Hiroshima Ryōri

岡山・広島料理

Okayama and Hiroshima are all on the Seto Inland Sea (Seto-naikai) in the far west of Honshū, Japan's main island. With their mild climate, they are good producers of all kinds of fish and vegetables.

Matsurizushi (Okayama)

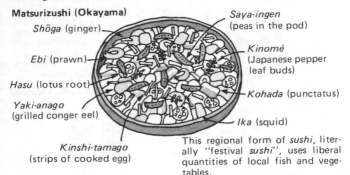

Shōga (ginger)

Ebi (prawn)

Hasu (lotus root)

Yaki-anago (grilled conger eel)

Kinshi-tamago (strips of cooked egg)

Saya-ingen (peas in the pod)

Kinomé (Japanese pepper leaf buds)

Kohada (punctatus)

Ika (squid)

This regional form of *sushi*, literally "festival *sushi*", uses liberal quantities of local fish and vegetables.

Mamakari-zuké (Okayama)

Mamakari-zuké, which literally means "rice-borrowing pickle", is made by pickling the *sappa* (pilchard), that can be caught from summer to autumn, in vinegar and *shōga* (ginger). The name implies that it must be eaten with plenty of rice, making it necessary to borrow.

Kaki-ryōri (Hiroshima)

Hiroshima is well-known for its *kaki* (oysters), a popular dish in winter. They are grilled in their shells and eaten with lemon or *miso* (fermented soy-bean paste) in the hotpot known as *doté-nabé* (see p. 32).

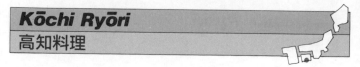

Kōchi Ryōri
高知料理

Kōchi, which faces the Pacific and has a hot and humid climate, is a famous *katsuo* (bonito) fishing port. Its culinary specialty is lavish arrangements of fish and vegetables designed to display the materials in as natural a way as possible.

Sawachi-ryōri

Sawachi-ryōri is the typical Kōchi cuisine served at parties and banquets. It consists of four dishes called *tsukuri*, *kumimono*, *sushi*, and *sunomono*, each arranged on large dishes 40 to 60 cm in diameter.

Kumimono

Kumimono is an assortment of foods usually eaten as *osechi-ryōri* (see p 60), such as *ebi* (prawn) wrapped in a *shiso* (beefsteak plant) leaf and fried; boiled crab; and boiled *sansai* (wild vegetables).

Sunomono

This dish consists mainly of *katsuo* lightly grilled, cooled, and pickled in vinegar and soy sauce seasoned with *ninniku* (garlic) and *shōga* . The dish is garnished with cucumber, *negi* (spring onions) and *myōga* (Japanese ginger).

Tsukuri

This consists of raw seasonal fish such as *katsuo*, *ika* (squid), and *kihada* (yellowfin tuna) cut and arranged *sashimi*-style.

Sushi

The *sushi* served as part of *sawachi-ryōri* consists of the usual *nigirizushi* (see p. 22) and *makizushi* (see p.26), plus *sugatazushi*, whole fish such as *amadai* (a variety of bream) and *saba* (mackerel) stuffed with *sushi* rice.

Nagasaki Ryōri
長崎料理

During the Edo era (from the 17th to the 19th century), Nagasaki flourished as the only port in Japan allowed to carry on trade with the outside world. Its contacts with Portugal, Holland and China produced the unique cuisine known as *shippoku-ryōri*.

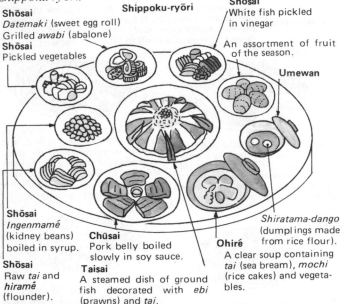

Shippoku-ryōri

Shōsai
Datemaki (sweet egg roll)
Grilled *awabi* (abalone)

Shōsai
Pickled vegetables

Shōsai
White fish pickled in vinegar

An assortment of fruit of the season.

Umewan

Shōsai
Ingenmamé (kidney beans) boiled in syrup.

Chūsai
Pork belly boiled slowly in soy sauce.

Shōsai
Raw *tai* and *hiramé* (flounder).

Taisai
A steamed dish of ground fish decorated with *ebi* (prawns) and *tai*.

Ohiré
A clear soup containing *tai* (sea bream), *mochi* (rice cakes) and vegetables.

Shiratama-dango (dumplings made from rice flour).

This style of cooking is used to entertain guests on special occasions. It consists of an assortment of different dishes served one by one on a large lacquered table. The meal starts with a clear soup called *ohiré* and continues with *shōsai* (small dishes), *chūsai* (medium-sized dishes) and *taisai* (large dishes) in that order, ending with a type of *shiruko* (sweet adzuki-bean soup) called *umewan,* and fruit.

Kagoshima Ryōri
鹿児島料理

Kagoshima, in the extreme south of **Kyūshū**, is located near the tropics. It is known for its pork dishes and as a producer of *shōchū* (see p. 142). Alcohol is used in many of Kagoshima's regional dishes, making them heavy and filling.

Tonkotsu-ryōri

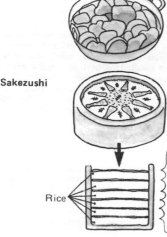

To make this dish, pork with the bone in is cut into pieces 4 to 5 cm thick, pan-fried in oil, and then stewed for 2 to 3 hours in a mixture of *shōchū*, *kurozatō* (brown sugar) and *miso* (see p.158).

Sakezushi

Sakezushi uses *saké*-seasoned rice, boiled vegetables, and fish pickled in vinegar. The rice and the other ingredients are arranged in alternate layers.

Rice

Takénoko (bamboo shoot) and *fuki* (bog rhubarb)

Kamaboko (boiled fish-paste cakes) and *ika* (squid)

Shiitaké (edible fungus) and *tamagoyaki* (omelette)

Tai (sea bream) pickled in vinegar

This regional specialty consists of raw *kibinago*, a cousin of the *iwashi* (sardine). It is eaten with *ponzu* (see p.30) or *sumiso* (*miso*-flavored vinegar). The best months for this dish are February and March.

Kibinago

Satsuma-agé

Satsuma-agé is prepared by mixing ground fish with wheat flour, shaping the mixture into pancakes and frying them. The fish used include *aji* (horse mackerel), *iwashi* (sardines) and *fuka* (a species of shark), etc.

Unusual Meat Dishes
珍しい肉料理

The types of meat most commonly eaten in Japan are beef, pork, and chicken. However, the meat of wild boar, horse, duck etc. is often used in regional cooking, and you can eat those unusual meat dishes in the big cities such as Tōkyō, Ōsaka, and etc.

Botan-nabé

Botan-nabé is a hotpot which uses the meat of the *inoshishi* (wild boar) sliced thinly and cooked with *miso* (fermented soy-bean paste), sugar, *saké*, and *mirin* (sweet *saké*). It is best during the winter months, from November to March. *Tōfu* (bean curd) and various vegetables, such as *daikon* (Japanese radish) and *hakusai* (Chinese cabbage) are used in the dish.

Sakura-nabé

Sakura-nabé consists of thinly-sliced *baniku* (horse meat) cooked *sukiyaki*-style on a hotplate with *shirataki* noodles (see p. 28) and *negi* (spring onions). It is usually eaten with a *miso*-flavored sauce rather than a soy-flavored one.

Basashi is raw horsemeat and only the best cuts of meat are used; those which contain a high proportion of fat and are known as *shimofuri* ("frosted") because of the marbled appearance the fat gives the meat. The meat is chewy but sweet-tasting, and is eaten thinly-sliced with grated *shōga* (ginger) and soy sauce.

Basashi

Kamo-no-sukiyaki

Kamo-no-sukiyaki is a duck-meat version of *sukiyaki* in which the meat is dipped in soy sauce and cooked on a thick hot-plate.

Okariba-yaki

Okariba-yaki, or hunters' grill, consists of the meat of small birds such as *suzumé* (sparrow) or *uzura* (quail) charcoal-grilled on skewers with pieces of *nasu* (eggplant), *pīman* (green bell pepper) or other vegetables. The sauce is either soy sauce and *mirin* based or a sweeter version using *miso*, depending on the locality. This dish is best from November to February.

Shika-no-sashimi

Shika-no-sashimi is raw deer meat. It is eaten with *sumiso*, made by mixing *miso* (fermented soy-bean paste) with *su* (rice vinegar), and is soft and light-tasting.

Ekiben
駅弁

Ekiben are the boxed lunches sold at stations and on trains all over Japan. They are a cheap and convenient way of trying some of the local specialties. The containers in which *ekiben* are sold are often designed to represent the particular regional dish that they feature. *Ocha* (green tea) in plastic containers is always sold to go with *ekiben*.

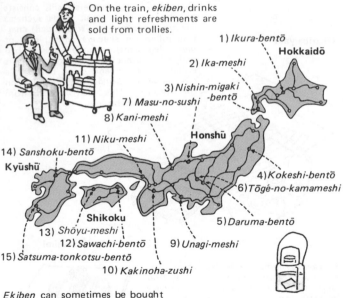

On the train, *ekiben*, drinks and light refreshments are sold from trollies.

1) *Ikura-bentō*
Hokkaidō
2) *Ika-meshi*
3) *Nishin-migaki -bentō*
7) *Masu-no-sushi*
8) *Kani-meshi*
11) *Niku-meshi*
14) *Sanshoku-bentō*
Kyūshū
Honshū
4) *Kokeshi-bentō*
6) *Tōgé-no-kamameshi*
5) *Daruma-bentō*
Shikoku
13) *Shōyu-meshi*
12) *Sawachi-bentō*
9) *Unagi-meshi*
15) *Satsuma-tonkotsu-bentō*
10) *Kakinoha-zushi*

Ekiben can sometimes be bought without leaving one's seat on the train.

Ocha (green tea) in a plastic container.

1) Ikura-bentō
Iwamizawa Station, Hakodaté Main Line

This *bentō* consists of *saké* (salmon) and *ikura* (salted salmon roe) on soy sauce-flavored rice.

2) Ika-meshi
Mori Station, Hakodaté Main Line

Ika-meshi is made by stuffing a whole *ika* (squid) with rice and cooking it in a sweet, spicy sauce. Each *bentō* contains two or three squid.

3) Nishin-migaki-bentō
Hakodaté Station, Hakodaté Main Line

This *bentō* features *nishin* (herring) boiled for a long time in a sweet, spicy sauce until the bones are soft enough to eat.

4) Kokeshi-bentō
Morioka Station, Tōhoku Shinkansen

This *bentō* is sold in a pottery container in the shape of a *kokeshi*, the ubiquitous wooden dolls that are a folk-craft specialty of the Tōhoku region.

5) Daruma-bentō
Takasaki Station, Jōetsu Shin-Kansen

This *bentō*, packed in a plastic container shaped like the *daruma* doll that *Takasaki* is famous for, contains mainly *sansai* (mountain vegetables). The container can be used as a money-box after the *bentō* has been eaten.

6) Tōgé-no-kamameshi
Yokokawa Station, Shin-etsu Line

This *bentō* consists of rice cooked in stock, garnished with chicken, *shiitaké*, *takenoko*, *gobō* (burdock root), *sansai*, *yudé-tamago* (boiled egg), and *kuri* boiled in syrup. It is served in an earthenware pot containing just enough for one person, with *tsukemono* in a separate container.

7) Masu-no-sushi
Toyama Station, Hokuriku Main Line

This colorful *bentō* contains *oshi-zushi* (see p.183) made with *masu* (trout) wrapped in a bamboo leaf and packed in a box made of *sugi* (Japanese cedar).

8) Kani-meshi
Fukui Station, Hokuriku Main Line

Kani-meshi is an excellent way of enjoying every part of the *zuwai-gani* (a large species of spider crab), a specialty of Fukui. The rice is flavored by cooking it together with the *ransō* (ovary) of the female crab, while the meat of the male crab is used as a garnish.

9) Unagi-meshi
Hamamatsu Station, Tōkaidō Shinkansen

This is a filling *bentō* consisting of a whole eel grilled *kabayaki*-style (see p. 40) on top of rice.

10) Kakinoha-zushi
Nara Station, Kansai Main Line

This *bentō* features five different kinds of *oshizushi* (see p.183) wrapped in a *kaki* (persimmon) leaf. The five kinds of *sushi* used are *shio-saba* (salted mackerel), *hiramé* (flounder), *masu* (trout), *kombu* (kelp) and *tai* (sea bream).

11) Niku-meshi
Shin-Kōbé Station, Tōkaidō Shinkansen

Niku-meshi consists of top-quality beef on rice, garnished with pineapple, olives, sour-sweet *umé-no-shisomaki* (Japanese apricot wrapped in a beefsteak plant leaf), and *nara-zuké* (vegetables pickled in *saké* lees). The beef is marinated in twelve different spices before being cooked.

12) Sawachi-bentō
Takamatsu Station, Yosan Main Line

This *bentō* is a sumptuous meal including both Japanese and Western delicacies such as *sushi*, chicken and fruit, in a box with four compartments.

13) Shōyu-meshi
Matsuyama Station, Yosan Main Line

This *bentō* consists of *gomoku-gohan* (literally, "five-item rice") prepared by mixing rice with chicken, carrot, *gobō* (burdock root), *shiitaké* (edible fungus), and *takénoko* (bamboo shoot), seasoning with soy sauce and cooking.

14) Sanshoku-bentō
Hakata Station, Tōkaidō·San-yō Shinkansen

Sanshoku-bentō is a three-tiered *bentō* with a black, a red, and a green layer. Each tier contains rice and accompaniments, and the whole box contains enough for two people.

15) Satsuma-tonkotsu-bentō
Nishi-kagoshima Station, Kagoshima Main Line

This *bentō* contains *tonkotsu*, a Kagoshima specialty made by stewing the ribs of the *kurobuta* (black pig) for a long time in *shō-chū* (see p.142), *miso* (fermented soy-bean paste) and *kurozatō* (brown sugar).

Yatai Snacks
屋台の食べ物

A common sight in the streets of Japanese towns and cities is the *yatai*, a mobile stall with a roof and cooking facilities, selling various types of food and drink. *Yatai* are often to be seen clustered around stations, parks and fairgrounds, or, on *ennichi* (festival days), in the grounds of shrines.

Okonomiyaki

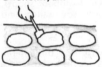

At *ennichi* (fairs), there will always be *yatai* (stalls) selling *okonomiyaki*, a round pancake made by mixing flour and water and cooking the mixture on a griddle, with vegetables, meat, egg, or seafood on the top. The *okonomiyaki* is brushed with sauce, folded double, and handed to the customers.

Takoyaki

Takoyaki are similar to *okonomiyaki* except that they are smaller and the filling consists of boiled octopus cut into pieces. Each *takoyaki* is about 3 cm in diameter, and seven to ten of them make one serving. They are handed to the customers on a plate and eaten with a *tsumayōji* (toothpick).

Wata-amé

Wata-amé, the equivalent of America's cotton candy or Britain's candy floss, is the spun sugar on a stick that children love. It is best eaten quickly, since it shrivels up after a few hours.

Rāmen

Many of the stalls that gather round stations in the business districts at night are *rāmen-ya*, serving bowls of hot *rāmen* noodles (see p.96), served in a soy sauce-flavored soup. Some of these stalls stay open as late as three or four a.m.

Steamed *chūka-men* (chinese noodles) are mixed with vegetables, meat, and plenty of sauce and cooked on a hot plate to make *yaki-soba*. They are served with the spicy red pickled ginger called *benishōga*, and *aonori* (seaweed flakes).

Yaki-soba

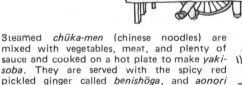

Oden

Oden (see p. 35) stalls appear on the streets in autumn and winter. Most of these have a few stools or upturned packing crates for the customers to sit on while they drink their beer, *saké* or *shōchū* and tuck into their *oden*. The *saké* served at *oden* stalls is usually *koppuzaké*, *saké* sold in individual glasses and drunk cold.

Ishiyaki-imo

The *ishiyaki-imo* (baked sweet potato) seller is a familiar sight in autumn and winter. Crying "*ishiyaki-imo*", he pulls his stall through the streets, selling *satsuma-imo* (sweet potatoes) baked by burying them in hot pebbles.

The price of *ishiyaki-imo* depends on the weight.

Tōmorokoshi
(corn-on-the-cob)

In Japan, corn-on-the-cob is usually grilled and brushed with soy sauce rather than being boiled. Some *yaki-imo* stalls also sell *tōmorokoshi*.

Hot-dogs and Frankfurters

Light vans equipped with kitchens on the back and selling hot dogs and frankfurters are a common sight. Help-yourself tubes of tomato ketchup and mustard are supplied.

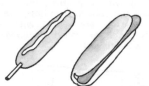

How to Eat Yatai Snacks

Rāmen and *oden* are eaten standing or sitting at the *yatai*, but *okonomiyaki* and *takoyaki* can be taken home to eat. *Okonomiyaki* and *takoyaki* used to be sold wrapped in thin sheets of wood called *kyōgi*, but these have now been replaced by styrofoam trays.

WATERSTONES WEST END

25/06/94 11:04   J   42   17309

```
   1 @  16.95 1859670105      £    16.95*
                POP-UP BOOK
SUBTOTAL                      £    16.95
SALES TAX @  0.00%            £     0.00
TOTAL                         £    16.95
TENDER BKTKN                  £    15.00
TENDER CASH                   £     2.00
CHANGE                        £     0.05
```

WATERSTONE'S BOOKSELLERS LTD.128 PRINCES
ST.EDINBURGH.031 226 2666.VAT:238554833

CONFECTIONERY & DRINKS

If you call western style confections with chocolate or cream an oil painting simple Japanese sweets can be called a Japanese water color or black ink drawing. Confectioners give full play to their power in making them. Try the combination of Japanese green-tea and sweets, and Japanese saké.

Nama-gashi

生菓子

Nama-gashi are sweet cakes made mainly from *mochi-gomé* (a glutinous kind of rice used for making *mochi*), wheat flour, *kanten* (agar-agar) and *an*, a paste made from sugar and beans. Their taste and appearance are carefully designed to match the seasons; and, as the term *nama* (uncooked) implies, they do not keep. They are eaten at tea-time with *ocha* (Japanese green tea) in the same way as Western cakes are eaten with tea.

Nerikiri

Neri-kiri represent the ultimate refinement of the art of *wa-gashi*. They are from white *koshi-an* mixed with *shira-tamako* (refined glutinous-rice flour) and coloured with *matcha*, egg yolk, etc. They are moulded in the shape of flowers, birds, and fruit, to represent the seasons, and are served mainly at the tea ceremony or on occasions of celebration.

Mushi-yōkan

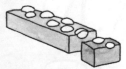

Mushi-yōkan is made by mixing *an* and wheat flour and steaming the mixture in a mould. It is a chewy form of *yōkan*, and it usually contains chestnuts.

Mizu-yōkan

Mizu-yōkan is made in a similar way to *neri-yōkan*, but it contains more water and is more jelly-like. It is often sold in cans, and is most refreshing when eaten chilled. It is popular in summer.

Neri-yōkan

Neri-yōkan is made from a mixture of adzuki-bean *koshi-an*, sugar, and *kanten*, shaped in a mould. It is very sweet, since it contains a lot of sugar, but it keeps for a long time.

Manjū

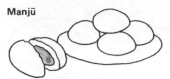

Monaka

Manjū, the most popular form of *wagashi*, are a kind of dumpling made from wheat flour and baking powder, filled with *an* and steamed.

Monaka is a kind of round or square double wafer filled with *an*. The round shape represents the full moon. *Monaka*, like *manjū*, are quite large and filling.

HOW TO MAKE KOSHI-AN

2) Pour beans onto the sieve and mash with a paddle, pouring water over little by little.

1) Bring to a boil and simmer *azuki* beans slowly till soft.

3) Pour the watery pulp onto *fukin* (cotton dish cloth) placed over another bowl.

5) Put this paste in a pan, add sugar, place over low heat and keep stirring till it becomes thick. Cool it down. This is sweetened bean paste — *koshi-an*.

4) Wring out all the water, the creamy remains in *fukin* is unsweetened, pured bean paste — *nama-an*.

Most *an* is made from *azuki* (adzuki beans). There are two further categories of *an* — *koshi-an*, which is smooth and is made by first removing the skins of the beans, and *tsubu-an*, which is chunky and in which the shape of the beans can still be seen.

Ohagi

Ohagi are eaten mainly at *higan*, the festival of the spring or autumn equinox. Steamed *mochi-gomé* (glutinous rice) is kneaded into a ball and wrapped in *azuki-an, kinako* (see p.148), or *goma* (sesame).

HOW TO MAKE OHAGI

1) Wash some *mochi-gomé* (glutinous rice) and ordinary white rice well. Place on a *zaru* (bamboo rack) and leave for half a day.

2) Add water to the rice and boil.

3) Place the rice in a *suribachi* and grind it with a *surikogi*.

Surikogi (wooden pestle)

Suribachi (earthenware mortar)

Azuki-an

Kinako (soy-bean flour)

Kuro-goma (black sesame)

5) Cover in *azuki-an, kinako* and *goma*.

4) Mold the rice into small egg shapes with the hands.

Sakura-mochi

 Cherry leaf

Sakura-mochi resemble small, pale-pink pancakes filled with *azuki-an*. They are wrapped in a cherry leaf pickled in brine. *Sakura-mochi* are always eaten at *Hina-matsuri,* the Doll's Festival, on the third of March.

Kuzu-zakura

Kuzu-zakura consist of *azuki-an* wrapped in a transparent jelly made from the root of the *kuzu* (kudzu, or arrowroot). They are eaten chilled in summer.

Kusa-mochi

Kusa-mochi are dumplings made from rice flour mixed with the boiled leaves of the *yomogi,* or mugwort. *Kusa-mochi* are green and are usually filled with *azuki-an.*

Azuki-an (bean jam)

Chimaki

Chimaki are sweet, soft, rice dumplings wrapped in bamboo leaves. Like *kashiwa-mochi,* they are eaten at Boys' Festival on the fifth of May.

Kashiwa-mochi

Kashiwa-mochi are rice-flour dumplings filled with *an* or *miso-an* (*shiro-an,* made from white kidney bean, mixed with *miso*), and wrapped in the leaf of the *kashiwa,* or oak tree. They are eaten at *Tango-no-Sekku* (Boy's Festival) on the fifth of May.

Daifuku

Daifuku are a very popular type of Japanese cake sold all the year round. They consist of a large quantity of *an* wrapped in a thin layer of *mochi.*

Kushi-dango

Bamboo stick

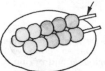

Kushi-dango are small rice-flour dumplings speared on a bamboo stick. They are eaten coated with *an,* or grilled on a wire rack and coated with a sticky sauce made from soy sauce and sugar.

Hi-gashi
干菓子

Hi-gashi are dried form of *wagashi* (Japanese cakes) made from rice, wheat, millet, sugar, and *mizu-amé* (glucose). Because of their low moisture content, they keep for a very long time. They are often molded into shapes representing the seasons, and are used in the tea ceremony.

Rakugan

Rakugan are made by steaming rice flour made from *mochi-gomé* (glutinous rice), mixing sugar with the dough, shaping it in wooden molds, and then drying it.

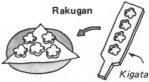

Kigata
(wooden molds)

Sembei

Nori
(dried seaweed)

Araré
(pellet-shaped *sembei*)

Sembei, or rice crackers, come in two types, sweet and savoury. The sweet kind are made by mixing wheat flour with sugar and *mizu-amé* and baking it, while the savoury kind are made by steaming rice flour, cutting it into shapes, baking it and brushing it with soy sauce.

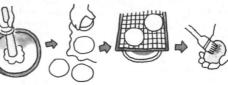

Satōzuké

Okoshi

Satōzuké are crystallized fruit and vegetables made by boiling the ingredients in syrup and then drying them.

Okoshi are cakes made by toasting rice, wheat, or millet, then mixing the toasted grain with syrup or *mizu-amé* and drying it.

Namban-gashi

南蛮菓子

Namban-gashi is the term used for the cakes made by the Spanish and Portuguese when they came to Japan in the 16th century. Now, these cakes have become a familiar part of Japanese life and are often eaten at teatime or given as presents.

Kasutera

Kasutera, the Japanese for "castella," is a type of sponge cake made from eggs, wheat flour, and sugar.

Bōro

Bōro are a kind of biscuit made from wheat flour, eggs, and sugar, baked hard. One kind of *bōro,* called *soba-bōro,* is made with *soba-ko* (buckwheat flour).

Kompeitō

Kompeitō are tiny sugar balls in the shape of horned spheres, made from syrup and corn starch.

Geppei, or moon cakes, originally came from China and consist of a pastry case made from wheat flour, sugar and lard, stuffed with fruit and nuts, *goma,* and *koshi-an* (see p. 129).

Geppei

Natsumé (jujubes, or Chinese dates)

Kurumi (walnuts)

Zatsu-gashi
雑菓子

Zatsu-gashi, miscellaneous snacks, include all kinds of everyday snacks for teatime and for children. They are easily purchased and less expensive than *nama-gashi* (unbaked cakes) or *hi-gashi* (dry confectionery) and go well with *bancha* and *hōjicha*.

Tai-yaki and Imagawa-yaki

Cooking molds

Both *tai-yaki* and *imagawa-yaki* are a kind of pancake stuffed with an, but *tai-yaki* are in the shape of the *tai,* or sea bream, a symbol of good luck in Japan, while *imagawa-yaki* are round.

Amanattō

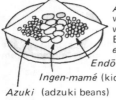

Ama-nattō consists of a variety of different whole beans boiled with sugar and sprinkled with a fine sugar coating like crystallized fruit. Beans used include *azuki, ingen-mamé,* and *endō-mamé.*

Endō-mamé (peas)

Ingen-mamé (kidney beans)

Azuki (adzuki beans)

—— **Notes on Buying Wagashi** ——

The best place to buy *wagashi*, especially *nama-gashi* and *hi-gashi*, is at one of the many special *wagashi* shops, but you can also buy them in the food departments of department stores. *Wagashi* are often given as presents, but if you are thinking of doing this, make sure you check with the shop assistant how long the *wagashi* will keep.

Karintō

Karintō is a hard, crunchy sweetmeat made by frying strips of wheat flour and egg and sugar mixture and sprinkling the strips with white or brown sugar.

Chitosé-amé

Literally "a thousand years candy", *chitosé-amé* is made by boiling down *mizu-amé* (glucose) and repeatedly pulling it out until it forms sticks. It is eaten at the festival of *Shichi-go-san,* a day of celebration for children aged three, five, and seven.

Daigaku-imo

Daigaku-imo, literally "college potatoes" are *satsuma-imo* (sweet potatoes) fried in oil, covered in a sweet, sticky coating, and sprinkled with *kuro-goma* (black sesame seeds).

HOW TO MAKE DAIGAKU-IMO

1) Cut some *satsuma imo* into irregular lumps.

2) Fry in oil.

3) Make syrup.

4) Turn off the heat, put in the fried *satsuma-imo,* and sprinkle with *kuro-goma.*

Water   Vinegar

Sugar   Soy sauce

Kammi-dokoro
甘味処

The *kammi-dokoro* is the traditional Japanese teashop. *Ocha* (green tea) is served and various sweet dishes which correspond to the Western dessert are available. People drop into the *kammi-dokoro* for a rest, a cup of tea, and a snack, and it is especially popular among young ladies.

In many *kammi-dokoro,* you can buy takeaway confectionery such as *ohagi* (see p. 130) and *kusa-dango* (see p.138).

To make *ammitsu,* cubes of *kanten* (see p.139) are placed in a dish with other ingredients such as *azuki-an, aka-endōmamé* (a kind of red pea), fruit, and served with syrup. Although served **cold,** this dish is eaten all the year round and is the most popular of the *kammi-dokoro's* specialties.

Ammitsu

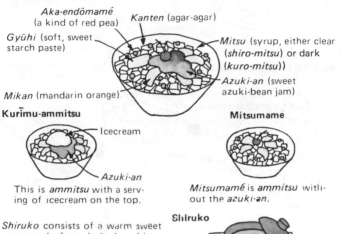

Aka-endōmamé (a kind of red pea) *Kanten* (agar-agar)

Gyūhi (soft, sweet starch paste)

Mitsu (syrup, either clear (*shiro-mitsu*) or dark (*kuro-mitsu*))

Azuki-an (sweet azuki-bean jam)

Mikan (mandarin orange)

Kurīmu-ammitsu

Icecream

Azuki-an

This is *ammitsu* with a serving of icecream on the top.

Mitsumame

Mitsumamé is *ammitsu* without the *azuki-an.*

Shiruko consists of a warm sweet soup made from boiled *azuki-an,* containing baked *mochi* (rice cakes). It is eaten with pickled *hojiso* (see p.156)

Shiruko

Hojiso

Zenzai

Azuki-an   *Mochi* (rice cakes)

Zenzai consists of baked *mochi* placed in a *wan* (bowl) with boiled *azuki-an* on the top. It is sweeter and more filling than *shiruko.*

Gozenjiruko: This is normal *Shiruko* made with *Koshi-an* (see p. 129).

Inakajiruko: This is *shiruko* made with *tsubu-an* (see p.129).

Abekawa-mochi

Abekawa-mochi consists of *mochi* (pounded rice cakes) coated in sweetened *kinako* (see p. 148).

Nihoncha (Green tea)

HOW TO MAKE ABEKAWA-MOCHI

The *mochi* are ready when they swell up.

Yu (hot water)

Mochi (pounded rice cake)

Ami (wire rack)

Sugar

Hibachi (charcoal brazier)

Kinako (soy-bean flour)

Kusa-dango

Tsubu-an

Tsubu-an

Isobemaki

Nori (dried seaweed)

Kusa-dango are small, round, rice-flour dumplings colored green with *yomogi* (mugwort) and coated with *tsubu-an* (see p. 129).

Isobemaki are made by grilling *mochi*, coating them with soy sauce and wrapping them in *nori* (dried seaweed).

138

Kanten

Kanten (agar-agar, or Japanese gelatin) looks like jelly but is actually made from seaweed.

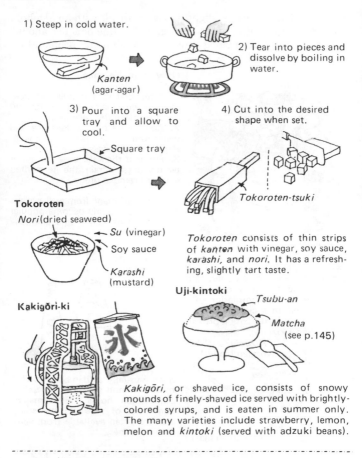

1) Steep in cold water.

Kanten
(agar-agar)

2) Tear into pieces and dissolve by boiling in water.

3) Pour into a square tray and allow to cool.

Square tray

4) Cut into the desired shape when set.

Tokoroten-tsuki

Tokoroten

Nori (dried seaweed)

Su (vinegar)

Soy sauce

Karashi (mustard)

Tokoroten consists of thin strips of *kanten* with vinegar, soy sauce, *karashi*, and *nori*. It has a refreshing, slightly tart taste.

Uji-kintoki

Tsubu-an

Matcha (see p.145)

Kakigōri-ki

氷

Kakigōri, or shaved ice, consists of snowy mounds of finely-shaved ice served with brightly-colored syrups, and is eaten in summer only. The many varieties include strawberry, lemon, melon and *kintoki* (served with adzuki beans).

Saké is a clear, colorless, slightly viscous drink with an alcohol content of 15-16%. It is sweet-tasting, with a fine bouquet, and is usually heated before being drunk, although many people also like to drink it cold.

How to make saké

1. After boiling the polished rice, blend it with malted rice, water and yeast to make the *saké* base.
2. Add boiled rice, malted rice and water to the *saké* base, and stir well. Repeat this process three times.
3. Ferment the *saké* base for about twenty days. Strain the fermented liquid to remove dregs.

"Junmaishu" made from well-polished rice has recently become popular because of its rich aroma and full-bodied flavor.

Komokaburi

Komokaburi are wooden *saké* casks wrapped in a rush mat. They are often used at ceremonies held to celebrate the start of a new company, or the completion of a new theater. In a custom known as *kagami-biraki*, the cask is broken open using a *kizuchi*.

Binzumé (bottling)

Kizuchi (wooden mallet)

Hishaku (ladle)

Wara (rush mat)

Saké is usually sold in bottles. The most common sizes are the *isshō-bin,* which holds 1.8ℓ. Smaller containers of *saké* are also sold, and are often available from vending machines.

Drinking vessels

Tokkuri
(*saké* flask)

Choko
(drinking cup)

Hakama
(bottle stand)

Saké is usually served in flasks called *tokkuri*, which hold about 0.18ℓ, carried in a small tray called *hakama*. It is drunk from little china or earthenware cups called *choko*.

Masu

Salt

The *masu*, a small wooden box which was formerly used for measuring out rice and beans, is now used as a drinking vessel for cold *saké*. A dab of salt is placed on the corner of the *masu* and tasted while drinking the *saké*.

Sakazuki

Sakazuki are the flat, shallow dishes used for drinking *saké* at weddings, on New Year's Day, or at other occasions of celebration. They are expensive, high-quality utensils made from lacquered wood.

Jizaké

Jizaké, or local *saké*, is the name given to the many different varieties of *saké* made in limited quantities in local districts rather than in large, centralized factories. Because of the different ingredients and processes used, *jizaké* has a unique taste reflecting the characteristics of the region where it is made.

HOW TO PREPARE KAN (HOT SAKÉ)

1) Pour the *saké* from the bottle into the *tokkuri*.

2) Place the *tokkuri* in boiling water and heat the *saké* to about 40°C (*nuru-kan*) or 50 – 60°C (*atsu-kan*).

3) Place the *tokkuri* in the *hakama*.

141

Shōchū
焼酎

Shōchū, Japan's answer to whisky and brandy, consists of distilled spirits made from a variety of raw materials. It is clear and colorless, like *saké*, but has a clean, dry taste.

Shōchū raw materials

Potato family:

Grains:

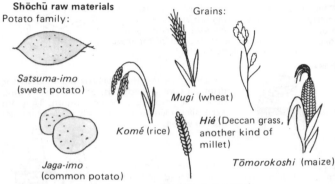

Satsuma-imo
(sweet potato)

Mugi (wheat)

Hié (Deccan grass, another kind of millet)

Komé (rice)

Tōmorokoshi (maize)

Jaga-imo
(common potato)

Awa (foxtail millet)

DRINKING SHŌCHŪ

Shōchū can be drunk straight, either "on the rocks" or heated, but it is usually drunk either mixed with hot water *(oyuwari)* or as a base for cocktails.

Oyuwari

Typical ratios of hot water to *shō-chū* are 5 : 5 *(gō-gō-wari)* or 6 : 4 *(roku-yon-wari)*.

Yu (hot water)

Shōchū

Chūhai

Lemon slice

Shōchū mixed with soda water and flavored syrup and served with ice and a slice of lemon, lime or other fruit is called *chūhai* (a contraction of "*shōchū* highball"). It is a cheap, refreshing long drink that has recently become very popular among young people.

Kajitsushu, or fruit liquor, is made by steeping various kinds of fruit in *shōchū* with sugar, thus sweetening the alcohol and imparting the flavor of the fruit to it. Japan's Liquor Tax Act allows all the kinds of fruit, but grapes, such as *umé* (Japanese apricots), strawberries, and plums to be used for this.

Since the *umé* or other fruit are used whole, a wide-mouthed glass jar is needed.

Shōchū

Howaito rikā (white liquor), a type of *shōchū* with an alcohol content of 35% is usually used.

Kōrizatō

Sugar is usually used in the form of *kōrizatō*, the most highly-refined form available, which comes in large, irregular lumps.

HOW TO MAKE UMESHU

1) Wash some fresh, green *umé*, and make a few holes in each with a bamboo skewer.

Kōrizatō

Umé (Japanese apricots)

Shōchū

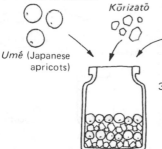

2) Place alternate layers of *umé* and *kōrizatō* in a wide-mouthed glass jar.

3) Finally, fill the jar with *shōchū*. Seal the jar tightly and store in a dark place. The longer you leave it, the more delectable your *umeshu* will become.

Sencha
煎茶

The Japanese drink *nihoncha* (Japanese tea) on many occasions: with meals, at teatime, and whenever a visitor calls. There are many kinds of *nihoncha,* but the variety known as *sencha* is the kind that is drunk most often. *Sencha* is made from soft, young tea leaves picked in May or June, and it has an excellent astringency and fragrance.

HOW TO MAKE SENCHA

1) Place the tea in the *kyūsu.*

Chagō
(tea scoop made
from split bamboo)

Kyūsu (teapot)

2) Pour freshly-boiled water into a *yutsubo* and allow it to cool to 60°C − 70°C.

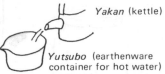

Yakan (kettle)

Yutsubo (earthenware container for hot water)

3) Pour the hot water into the *kyūsu*, replace the lid, and allow to stand for about 1 minute.

4) Pour into heated *chawan.*

Chataku (tea-table)

Bancha

Bancha is made from the large tea leaves picked in August, after the young leaves for *sencha* have been taken. It is made with boiling water.

Hōjicha

Hōjicha, a tea with an excellent aroma, is made by toasting *bancha* over a strong flame. It is drunk in the same way as *bancha.*

Yunomi
(large teacup)

144

Matcha, Gyokuro & Kawaricha

抹茶・玉露・変わり茶

Matcha and *gyokuro* are top-quality teas made by covering the young leaves that come out in May with straw to protect them from the sunlight. *Matcha* is not a tea that is drunk every day, but it is indispensable to the tea ceremony.

Matcha (powdered green tea)

Chasen (bamboo tea whisk)

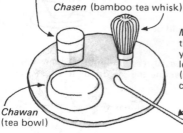

Matcha is made by removing the stalks from specially-grown young leaves and grinding the leaves to powder in an *usu* (mortar). It is a brilliant green color.

Chawan (tea bowl)

Chashaku (bamboo teaspoon)

HOW TO MAKE MATCHA

1) Using a *chashaku,* place 2 spoonfuls of *matcha* in a heated *chawan*.

Hishaku (ladle)

3) Holding the *chawan* steady with one hand, whisk the tea with a *chasen* until a fine foam is produced.

2) Pour hot water into the bowl using a *hishaku*.

Iced green tea

Iced green tea can be made by adding sugar to *matcha* and mixing it with cold water and ice. It is a clear, bright-green color.

Gyokuro

Gyokuro, which has a strong natural sweetness, is drunk in small quantities from a special, small *chawan*. Freshly-boiled water that has been allowed to cool to 40 — 50°C should be used.

Kawaricha

Kawaricha is the name given to special teas drunk at different seasons and on different occasions to celebrate the season, or to express congratulations or a wish.

Sakurayu

Sakurayu is hot water with salted cherry blossoms floating in it to represent spring. It is often drunk at weddings or engagement parties.

Ofukucha

Umeboshi (pickled Japanese apricot)

Kombu (kelp)

Ofukucha (literally, "tea of happiness") is a mixture of *bancha* (see p.144), *kombu, umeboshi,* etc. It is drunk at New Year and *Setsubun,* the beginning of spring according to the old Chinese calendar.

Storing Tea

Nihoncha is easily damaged by humidity, and the Japanese have devised various ways of storing their tea and preserving its natural color, taste, and fragrance. Shops store it in unglazed earthenware urns *(cha-tsubo)* or tin-lined wooden boxes *(cha-bako),* while at home it is kept in special canisters called *chazutsu.*

INGREDIENTS
&
SEASONINGS

The distinction of Japanese
cooking is to make the best use of
materials, so fresh and pretty
materials are necessary. Japanese
people are lucky enough to
have plenty of vegetables and
sea foods.

Soybean Products

大豆加工品

The Japanese have traditionally obtained their protein mainly from fish and soybeans. Soybeans are used to make a variety of foods indispensable to a proper Japanese meal, and these foods have gained in popularity recently as people have begun once again to appreciate their good qualities.

Nattō

Nattō is made by adding a yeast known as *nattō-kin* to boiled soybeans and allowing them to ferment. *Nattō* is eaten after being mixed with soy sauce and *negi* (spring onions) and served on top of boiled rice.

Yuba

Kinako

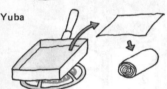

Yuba, dried bean curds, is made by boiling soya milk, skimming the curds off the top, and drying them. It is often used in soups or *nimono*.

Kinako is a powder made by roasting and grinding soybeans. It is used to coat *mochi* or *wagashi*.

Okara

Tō-nyū

Okara is a bean curd by-product and is cooked with vegetables.

Tō-nyū is soybean milk and is one of the ingredients of *tōfu*.

Tōfu, or bean curd, is made by solidifying soya milk with a coagulating agent called *nigari*. There are two kinds of *tōfu*: *kinugoshi* is soft and smooth, while *momen* is rougher-textured and more resilient. *Tōfu* is used extensively in soups, *nimono* (stewed foods) and *nabemono*.

Tōfu

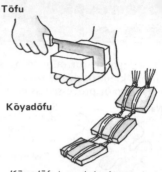

Yakidōfu

Yakidōfu is made by grilling fresh *tōfu*, thus reducing the moisture content and allowing it to keep a little longer. It is an indispensable ingredient in *sukiyaki* and other *nabemono* dishes.

Kōyadōfu

Kōyadōfu is made by freeze-drying *tōfu*, and, unlike fresh *tōfu*, it can be kept for a long time. It is softened by soaking in water and is then used in *nimono* and other dishes.

Atsu-agé

Abura-agé

Atsu-agé is made by frying *tōtu* lightly in oil. It is either eaten as it is, with the addition of soy sauce and other condiments, or used as an ingredient in *nimono*.

Since *abura-agé* is made by frying thin slices of *tōfu* in oil, it is very similar to *atsu-agé*. It is used to form the casing for the popular form of *sushi* known as *inarizushi*.

Gammodoki

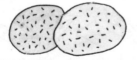

This dish, made by frying *tōfu* with *yama-imo* (yam) and other vegetables, was popular among priests in the days when eating meat was forbidden. It is said to taste like wild goose; hence the name, which literally means "like wild goose". It is a common ingredient of *oden*.

Since Japan is surrounded by sea, seaweeds are often used for various kinds of dishes such as a fresh seaweed salad, cooked in *miso* soup or processed as *nori*.

Wakamé

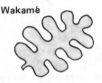

Salted fresh *wakamé* and dried *wakamé* are sold. Both of them have to be soaked in water before cooking. Salted fresh *wakamé* will triple in size where as dried *wakame* swells 10 times or more.

Dishes with Wakamé

Wakamé-no-miso-shiru
Softened and chopped *wakamé* in *miso* soup.

Sunomono

Wakamé seaweed is mixed with sliced cucumber, *udo* and a sauce of vinegar, sugar and salt.

Wakatakeni

A kind of spring dish in which *wakamé* seaweed is cooked with bamboo shoots in a broth of soy sauce and sugar.

Nori

Nori seaweed, made of *asakusanori,* appears on the table most often, since it goes well with rice. Other varieties of *nori* that you will come across in this book are: *hoshi-nori* (sundried), *yaki-nori* (toasted) and *ajitsuké-nori* (brushed with soy sauce and *mirin*, or sweet *saké*).

Toast *nori* seaweed by holding a sheet and passing only one side over a gas flame for 2 or 3 seconds to improve its flavor and texture.

Cut a standard sheet of *nori* into about 8 pieces, dip it in soy sauce and eat it with warm rice.

Sushi rice with a cooked egg and *kampyō* (see p.153) rolled in a sheet of *nori* is called *norimaki*.

Kombu (kelp)

Kombu is used for making stock, *nimono* (stewed foods) or *tsukudani* (see p.111). It is sold as dry sheets with high quality being shiny black in color.

Kobumaki

Rolled small fish (dried sardine) in softened *kombu* (soaked in water) are cooked in a broth of soy sauce. This is called *kobumaki*.

Kombu-no tsukudani

Small pieces of *kombu* cooked in a broth of soy sauce and *mirin* (sweet *saké*) for a long time is called *kombu-no-tsukudani*.

HOW TO MAKE KOMBU DASHI (KOMBU STOCK)

1) Wipe *kombu* lightly with a damp cloth and make several slits on each side.

3) Remove the *kombu* just before the water boils.

2) Fill a pot with cold water and put the *kombu* in it.

Hijiki (brown algae)

Hijiki, when sold, is brownish black, dried and 1 to 2 cm. long. Soak it in water for half an hour before cooking. The amount of *hijiki* will triple from the absorption of water. Fry it with oil and cook with *abura-age* (fried *tōfu*), carrots and soybeans.

Kanten (agar-agar)

Kanten is a freeze-dried form of cooked *tengusa* (heavenly grass), which is used for *mitsu-mamé, tokoroten,* and *yōkan*.

Tosaka-nori	Sugi-nori	Ogo-nori

They are sold fresh, but salted. Remove the salt with water before using in a salad or as a garnish for *sashimi*.

Kambutsu are keepable dried fish or vegetables. Soak them in water to soften them before cooking or using. The soaking water can be used as a basic seasoning to produce the relished flavor of Japanese cooking.

Katsuo-bushi
(dried bonito)

Katsuo-bushi is bonito that has been steamed, smoked and dried to woodlike hardness. It is then shaved into flakes using a bonito shaver. Packaged dried bonito flakes are available at stores. *Katsuobushi* gives great flavor to clear soup and simmered foods. It can also be sprinkled over boiled vegetables.

Niboshi (small dried sardines)

Small boiled and sun-dried sardines are *niboshi*. It's mostly used for fish stock which is made by just soaking then in cold water overnight without boiling.

Hoshi-shiitaké

Hoshi-shiitaké are dried brown mushrooms. To soften, they must be soaked in tepid water. They are cooked with soy sauce and sugar as an ingredient of *chirashizushi* or cooked with other vegetables in *nimono*. The soaking water has a good flavor so it's used for *shōjin-ryōri*.

There are two kinds of *hoshi-shiitaké*, one is called *donko* whose meat is thick and has a round shape; the other is called *kōshin* which is the opposite of *donko* being thin and flat.

Kōshin   Donko

Kampyō (dried gourd strips)

Bottle gourd flesh is shaved and dried into long ribbonlike strips. To soften, first knead strips in salt and wash in water then boil until soft. *Kampyō* has two uses; as a filling in such foods as *makizushi* (rolled *sushi*) and as something decorative to tie or fasten such foods as *kobumaki* (*kombu* roll), taking advantage of its long form.

Yaki-fu (baked wheat gluten)

Fu (wheat gluten) is made from gluten flour. *Yaki-fu* is baked wheat gluten and has a rather bland crispy texture.

Kyō-fu

Kyōka-fu

Shōnai-fu

These are made in a great variety of shapes, such as, flowers or mushrooms as shown. These can be used as ingredients in hot clear soup or by squeezing and soaking in hot water, used for *sunomono* (vinegared foods) with cucumbers.

Kuruma-fu (wheel wheat gulten)

Kuruma-fu has a shape of a wheel which has a diameter of about 8cm. To soften, soak in water, squeeze out the water and use as an ingredient in *sukiyaki*, or *tamagotoji* in which *fu* is cooked in soy sauce and covered with an egg.

Fish Paste Products

練り製品

This is a way of preserving large quantities of obtained fish. Grind the fish first, add seasonings and wheat flour to it then steam or deep-fry. This can be roasted, used as an *oden* ingredient or eaten as it is.

FISHES FOR MAKING PASTE PRODUCTS

The fish which are obtained in large quantity or large in size, or white fish which do not taste good when raw or grilled are: walley pollack, flying fish, shark, croaker to name a few.

Kamaboko

Kamaboko is the fish paste which is pasted on to a Japanese cedar before steaming.

In addition to the planked *kamaboko (ita-kamaboko)* there are a few more types such as:

Yaki-kamaboko, which is grilled and basted with sweet cooking *saké.*

Kobumaki-kamaboko, which is rolled inside *kombu* (see p.151) and steamed.

Sasa-kamaboko, which has a shape of a bamboo leaf

Hampen

The fish paste is mixed with *yama-imo* (yam) before boiling. The boiled paste, which is white and has marshmallow-like softness, is called *hampen.*

Datemaki

Datemaki is the fish paste which has a sweet taste because of the added eggs and sugar. The mixed paste is grilled. This is one of the popular traditional Japanese New Year foods *osechi-ryori*.

Chikuwa (literally bamboo wheels)

The fish paste is molded around a stainless steel rod (originally, a thin segment of bamboo stalk) before steaming. The steamed paste is grilled. This is often used as an *oden* ingredient.

Satsuma-age

The fish paste is made into a round shape then deep-fried. Some of them have chopped burdock, carrots and squid in them. To eat, grill them and dip in soy sauce, or use them in *oden*.

Fish Meat Ham and Sausages

Seasonings and fat are added to red meat fish paste such as *maguro* (tuna) to make ham and sausages. These are more crisp and simple in taste than the ones made of other meats.

Vegetables

野菜

Such vegetables as *shiso*, *kinomé*, and *mitsuba* are a necessary addition for seasonal food, and have a unique flavor and fragrance. Small amounts of these vegetables are used with *soba*, *sashimi*, or *nabemono*.

Shiso

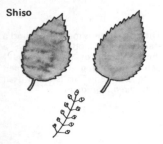

The green *shiso* that often appears as a garnish for *sashimi*, also is a *tempura* vegetable. Red *shiso* is used mainly in making *umeboshi* (pickled Japanese apricots) to add its red color and aroma. *Hojiso* is scraped off the stem with chopsticks or fingers and mixed into a dipping sauce. They are often used as a garnish for *sasimi* or *sunomono* (vinegared foods). Their natural season is summer.

Shōga (ginger)

Shōga has a fresh sharp flavor. *Fudé-shōga* which has a long slender stalk with a pink brush at the bottom, is marinated in sweetened vinegar and served with grilled fish, so it brings out more of the fish's flavor. Ground *hiné-shōga* is often used as a spicy condiment for *sōmen* (see p. 95) or is cooked with fish that has a strong odor to eliminate it.

Negi (spring onions)

Negi is available the year round in Japan, but the flavor of *negi* is best in winter since it has not only spicy hotness, but also sweetness. Sliced *negi* can't miss as one of the spicy condiments for *soba*, also one of the most usable vegetables for *nabemono* (hotpot dishes).

Kinomé

The Japanese prickly ash, or *sanshō* sends out new leaves in early spring. These aromatic and colorful young leaves enliven soups and simmered foods by being used as a garnish associated with spring.

Takenoko-no-kinomé-aé

This is a most symbolic spring food. Boiled bamboo shoots are dressed with light green *miso* flavored with ground *kinomé*.

Mitsuba

Mitsuba (trefoil) is a member of the parsley family, but its flavors are more between sorrel and celery. Two types of *mitsuba* are available in Japan; one is *ito-mitsuba* (thread trefoil), the other is *ne-mitsuba* (root trefoil).

Ito-mitsuba has a threadlike thin green stem. Used fresh and roughly chopped, it is added to soups or *chawan-mushi* (see p.172).

Ne-mitsuba which is fatter than *ito-mitsuba*, is lightly boiled, then served with soy sauce as *ohitashi*.

Hamabōfū

Hamabōfū is similar to *mitsuba* in shape, but its flavor and aroma are slightly lighter. Its stem is red and approximately 10cm long, which is cut open, criss-crossed and soaked in water, then shaped into an anchor and added to *sashimi* as a garnish.

Oroshiki (Graters)

Some of Japanese fresh spices are grated to bring out their fragrance. So, for Japanese cooking, graters are necessary. Graters are made of stainless steel, aluminum or plastic while traditional material is pottery.

Shōyu (soy sauce) and *miso* represent Japanese seasonings. They are made by fermenting rice, wheat, barley or beans. The fermented paste is allowed to mature for months or even up to three years in order to draw out its flavor.

Miso

Miso is made by crushing boiled soybeans and adding salt and *kōji* (malted rice which acts as a yeast) made from rice, wheat, barley or beans. The type of *kōji* determine the type of *miso*.

GEOGRAPHICAL DISTRIBUTION OF MISO

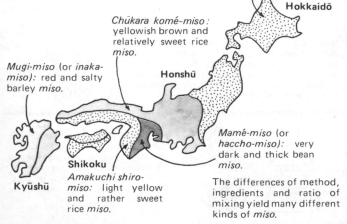

You will enjoy the wide variety of their flavor, aroma, color and texture.

Karakuchi komé-miso: light brown and salty rice *miso*.

Hokkaidō

Chūkara komé-miso: yellowish brown and relatively sweet rice *miso*.

Mugi-miso (or inaka-miso): red and salty barley *miso*.

Honshū

Mamé-miso (or haccho-miso): very dark and thick bean *miso*.

Shikoku

Kyūshū

Amakuchi shiro-miso: light yellow and rather sweet rice *miso*.

The differences of method, ingredients and ratio of mixing yield many different kinds of *miso*.

Shōyu (soy sauce)

Soy sauce is used most often among seasonings, as you can see it in *sukiyaki* and *donburimono* or as a dipping sauce for *sushi* and *sashimi*. It can be said that the taste of soy sauce reflects Japanese cuisine.

A mixture of steamed soybeans and roasted wheat is inoculated with *kojikin* (aspergillus mold). The resulting culture is mixed with brine. This mash is transferred to fermentation tanks for brewing.

Ingredients of Soy Sauce

Sugar

White sugar is most often used for cooking.

Japanese people's favorite is a sweet and salty taste made by mixing soy sauce and sugar. Sugar is used in *wagashi* (Japanese confectionery) as well.

Brown sugar is used for making the syrup for *ammitsu* and *kuzukiri*. Both are Japanese sweet snacks. (see p.137).

Kōrizatō (sugar candy) is used for making fruit liquor (see p.143).

Zaramé (crystal sugar) is used for candy, confectionery.

Granulated sugar is used for coffee, tea or western style confectionery. Also, for making the shape of sea bream or rose for celebrations.

Su (rice vinegar)

Rice vinegar is used for *sushi* and *sunomono*. Japanese produce rice vinegar which has strong acidity and flavor. Such vinegar dressings as *nihaizu* (two-flavors-vinegar, made by adding soy sauce), *sanbaizu* (three-flavors-vinegar, made by adding soy sauce and sugar) are often used for *sunomono*.

Saké and Mirin

Besides drinking *saké*, it is used as a seasoning to add relish to cooked food. *Mirin* is heavily sweetened *saké* used only in cooking to add a mild sweetness or to glaze grilled foods.

Ichimi tōgarashi

The entire hot red chili peppers *(taka-no-tsume,* talons of a hawk) including seeds and skin are ground into a coarse sort of pepper. This pepper resembles cayenne pepper. It is used in hot *soba,* or on pickled Chinese cabbage as a spicy condiment.

Wasabi (Japanese horseradish)

Since fresh *wasabi* (see p. 94) is expensive and difficult to preserve, powdered western horseradish is used. Powdered *wasabi* comes in small tins or packages. To prepare, add a small amount of tepid water to a small amount of powder. Mix until smooth. A paste *wasabi* comes ready-to-use in tubes.

Karashi

Karashi are the powdered seeds of the mustard plant. Japanese mustard is not as fragrant nor as mild as western mustard. To prepare, mix a small amount of Japanese mustard with a little bit of water. It is used sparingly with *oden* (see p.35) as a condiment.

HOW TO PREPARE POWDERED WASABI AND KARASHI

Mix Japanese *wasabi* or *karashi* powder with a bit of water to a stiff paste in the bottom of a small bowl and invert it for a while till the *wasabi* or *karashi* flavor ripens.

Sanshō

Kinomě, the leaves of the *sanshō* tree, are used in soup and dressed foods. The pod of the same tree is made into a powdered spice which is tangy, but not hot. It is used to counter fatty taste in such grilled foods as *yakitori* (see p.46) and *kabayaki* (see p. 40).

Goma

Kuro-goma   **Shiro-goma**
(black sesame) (white sesame)

Both black and white sesame seeds are very nourishing since they contain more than 50 percent oil. To grind, first lightly roast the seeds until they begin to crackle, then grind them in a mortar until flaky and aromatic.

A FEW SIMPLE RECIPES

Japanese dishes look
and sound easy, but difficult to cook. If you have basic
knowledge of Japanese cooking
and how seasonings are used,
they make your meal more
enjoyable. Let us introduce
the easiest style of cooking
here. We hope you'll
enjoy cooking it too.

How to Cook Rice
ご飯の炊き方

Ingredients (serves 5)
Komé (uncooked rice): 3 cups
Water: 3.3 cups

Gohan (cooked rice) is prepared by steaming it until it is soft and fluffy, without adding any seasoning.

Washing the rice:

1) Rub the rice about five times using the palm of the hand, and then rinse in cold water.

2) Leave the rice in the colander for 30 minutes to 1 hour to allow it to absorb the water.

Cooking the rice:

3) Put the rice in a *denki-gama* (electric rice cooker), add water, and switch on.

4) Leave to steam for 10 minutes after turning off the heat. Stir the rice with a moistened *shamoji* (spatula).

If you have no rice cooker, put the rice and the water in a thick pot and heat over a high flame. When the water boils, turn down the heat and cook for 20 minutes, then turn off the heat.

Hijiki-no-nitsuké
ひじきの煮つけ

Ingredients (serves 4)

Hijiki (brown algae):	40g
Abura-agé (fried *tōfu*):	2 sheets
Soy sauce:	4 tablespoons
Sugar:	2 tablespoons
Saké:	2 tablespoons
Oil.	1 tablespoon

This is a typical Japanese simmered dish in which keepable dried *hijiki* (see p.151) is used.

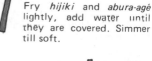

Drain off the water.

Soak *hijiki* in water for 15 minutes.

Fry *hijiki* and *abura-agé* lightly, add water until they are covered. Simmer till soft.

Pour hot water onto *abura-agé* to remove excess oil.

Cut *abura-agé* into 2 x 0.5 cm pieces.

Soy sauce   Sugar

Saké

Add soy sauce, sugar and *saké,* simmer another 10 minutes.

163

Sukiyaki

すき焼

Ingredients (serves 4)		Stock	
Thinly-sliced beef :	400g	*Dashi* (stock):	2/3 cup
Yaki-dōfu (grilled *tōfu*):	1 block	Soy sauce:	1/3 cup
Shiitaké (edible fungus):	8	*Mirin* (sweet *saké*):	1/3 cup
Negi (spring onions):	3	Sugar:	2 tablespoons
Beef fat:	50g		
Shirataki (noodles made from devil's-tongue starch):	2 packets		
Shungiku (edible chrysanthemum leaves):	200g		

1) Making the stock
Put the seasonings of the stock into a pan and heat until just boiling.

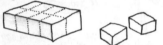

2) Cut the grilled *tōfu* into 8 equal-sized pieces.

3) Cut the *shirataki* into about 10 cm lengths.

4) Cut the *shungiku* into about 7 cm lengths.

5) Cut the *negi* into about 5 cm lengths.

6) Heat a hotplate and melt the beef fat on it. Fry the thinly-sliced beef lightly in the fat.

7) When the beef is browned, add the other ingredients plus the stock, and boil.

8) Eat the *sukiyaki* with a beaten raw egg.

Katsu-don
カツ丼

Ingredients (serves 1)		Sauce	
Pork:	1 slice	*Dashi* (stock):	1/2 cup
Koromo (batter):		Soy sauce:	1-1/2 tablespoon
flour, egg, breadcrumbs,		*Mirin* (sweet *saké*):	1 tablespoon
Onions:	1/4	Sugar:	1/4 tablespoon
Eggs:	1		

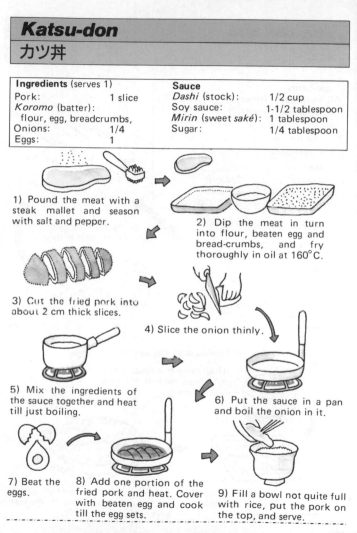

1) Pound the meat with a steak mallet and season with salt and pepper.

2) Dip the meat in turn into flour, beaten egg and bread-crumbs, and fry thoroughly in oil at 160°C.

3) Cut the fried pork into about 2 cm thick slices.

4) Slice the onion thinly.

5) Mix the ingredients of the sauce together and heat till just boiling.

6) Put the sauce in a pan and boil the onion in it.

7) Beat the eggs.

8) Add one portion of the fried pork and heat. Cover with beaten egg and cook till the egg sets.

9) Fill a bowl not quite full with rice, put the pork on the top, and serve.

Yakizakana
焼き魚

Ingredients

Aji-no-shioyaki (serves 1)
Aji (horse mackerel): 1
Salt: 1/2 teaspoon

Buri-no-teriyaki (serves 4)
Buri (yellowtail): 4 fillets

Sauce
Soy sauce: 1/2 cup
Mirin (sweet *saké*): 1/2 cup
Saké: 3 tablespoons

Aji-no-shioyaki (grilled fish)

1) Remove the *zeigo* (the part shown by the arrow) and gut the fish.

2) Score both sides of the fish and sprinkle with salt.

3) Place the fish on a metal mesh and grill both sides over a strong flame.

Buri-no-teriyaki (fish broiled with soy sauce)

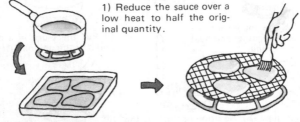

1) Reduce the sauce over a low heat to half the original quantity.

2) Cool the sauce, cover the fish with it, and leave for ten minutes.

3) Grill the fish briefly, brush with sauce, and grill again. Repeat this two or three times.

Nizakana

煮魚

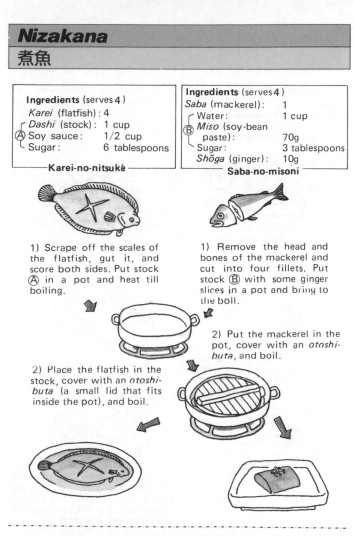

Ingredients (serves 4)
Karei (flatfish): 4
Ⓐ ⌈ *Dashi* (stock): 1 cup
 │ Soy sauce: 1/2 cup
 └ Sugar: 6 tablespoons

Karei-no-nitsuké

Ingredients (serves 4)
Saba (mackerel): 1
Ⓑ ⌈ Water: 1 cup
 │ *Miso* (soy-bean
 │ paste): 70g
 │ Sugar: 3 tablespoons
 └ *Shōga* (ginger): 10g

Saba-no-misoni

1) Scrape off the scales of the flatfish, gut it, and score both sides. Put stock Ⓐ in a pot and heat till boiling.

1) Remove the head and bones of the mackerel and cut into four fillets. Put stock Ⓑ with some ginger slices in a pot and bring to the boil.

2) Put the mackerel in the pot, cover with an *otoshi-buta*, and boil.

2) Place the flatfish in the stock, cover with an *otoshi-buta* (a small lid that fits inside the pot), and boil.

Tamago-yaki
卵焼き

Ingredients (serves 4)

Eggs:	4
Stock:	4 tablespoons
Sugar:	2 tablespoons
Soy sauce:	1 teaspoon
Salad oil	

To make *tamago-yaki*, a seasoned egg mixture is cooked in salad oil while being rolled over and over.

Soy sauce
Sugar

1) Break the eggs into a bowl and beat them, stirring in the stock and other seasonings.

2) Heat a *tamago-yaki* pan.

3) Put a small amount of salad oil in the pan and pour in 1/4 of the egg mixture.

4) Roll the egg mixture over gently from the edges.

5) Wipe the pan with a cloth soaked in salad oil.

6) Pour in 1/3 of the remaining egg mixture and roll it over several times. Repeat this process twice more, cut the resulting egg roll into slices, and serve.

Yudōfu & Hiya-yakko
湯豆腐・冷奴

Ingredients (serves 4)

Tōfu (bean curd): 2 blocks
Negi (spring onions):
Shōga (ginger): a small amount for seasoning
Kezuribushi (dried bonito shavings):
Kombu (kelp) a 20 cm-long piece

Tōfu should be put in a bowl full of ice water as soon as possible after it is bought.

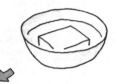

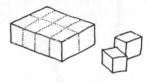

Cut each block of *tōfu* into eight equal-sized pieces.

Hiya-yakko

Shōga

Yudōfu

Put the *kombu* and *tōfu* in water in a pot, heat until the water boils, and eat straight away.

kombu

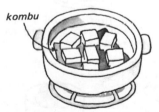

Put the *tōfu* in cold water in a bowl.

In both these dishes, the *negi*, *shōga* and *kezuribushi* are mixed with soy sauce to taste, and the *tōfu* is dipped in the mixture before being eaten.

169

Nikujaga
肉じゃが

Ingredients (serves 4)

Thinly-sliced beef:	150g
Potatoes:	4
Carrots:	1/2
Onions:	1
Water:	2 cups
Soy sauce:	4 tablespoons
Sugar:	2 tablespoons
Saké:	3 tablespoons

2) Cut the carrot into small rings and the onion into slices about 5 mm thick.

Beef

1) Peel the potatoes, cut them into bite-sized pieces and wash them in cold water.

3) Heat some oil in a pan and brown the meat and vegetables.

4) Pour in the water and add the *saké* and other seasonings after the flames have died down.

5) Stew for about 15 minutes, stirring occasionally.

6) Fill individual *chū-bachi* (medium-sized bowls) and serve.

Kimpira-gobō
きんぴらごぼう

Ingredients (serves 4)

Gobō (burdock root):	1
Carrot:	1/2
Aka-tōgarashi (red pepper):	1
Sesame oil:	2 tablespoons
Soy sauce:	4 tablespoons
Sugar:	2 tablespoons
Saké:	2 tablespoons

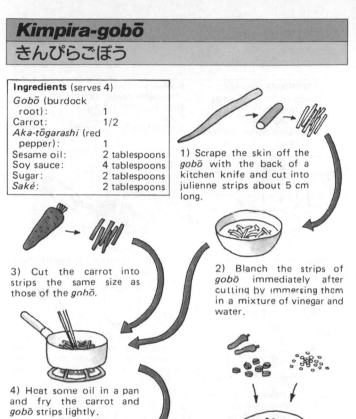

1) Scrape the skin off the *gobō* with the back of a kitchen knife and cut into julienne strips about 5 cm long.

3) Cut the carrot into strips the same size as those of the *gobō*.

2) Blanch the strips of *gobō* immediately after cutting by immersing them in a mixture of vinegar and water.

4) Heat some oil in a pan and fry the carrot and *gobō* strips lightly.

5) When the carrot and *gobō* have softened, add the *saké* and other seasonings. Turn down the heat and cook slowly.

6) Place in a small dish, garnish with rounds of red pepper, and sprinkle with *shirogoma* (white sesame seeds).

Chawan-mushi
茶碗蒸し

Ingredients (serves 4)		
Chicken:	40g	*Kamaboko* (boiled fish-paste cake): 30g
Ebi (prawns):	4	*Mitsuba* (trefoil): 5g
Nama-shiitaké (undried edible *shiitaké* fungus):	4	Eggs: 2
		Dashi(stock): 2 cups
		Salt: 1/2 teaspoon
		Soy sauce: 1 teaspoon

1) Mix the stock, salt and soy sauce, and stir in a beaten egg.

2) Strain the egg mixture.

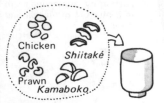

3) Cut the chicken, *shiitaké* and *kamaboko* into bite-sized pieces, peel the prawns, and put all these ingredients into a *chawan* for *chawan-mushi*.

4) Pour the egg mixture carefully into the *chawan* until it is seven-tenths full. Decorate the top with *mitsuba* cut into about 2 cm lengths.

5) Put the lid on the *chawan* and place it in a hot steamer. Steam at high heat for one or 2 minutes and then on low heat for a further about 15 minutes.

SUPPLEMENT

Japanese dishes
sound like they require
strict manner, but that's not
true. You have to know some of
the taboos, though. "When in
Rome, do as the Romans
do." We hope you'll
enjoy them too.

Use of Chopsticks & Tableware

箸・食器の使い方

Japanese food is eaten with chopsticks (*hashi*), and the most efficient way of using these handy little tools is to wield them in one hand, while lifting the dishes containing the food in the other. Along with the correct method of holding the chopsticks, this practice has developed over the years into a precept of proper table etiquette.

HOW TO HOLD CHOPSTICKS PROPERLY

Hold the chopsticks slightly towards the thick end. Keeping the lower chopstick steady, move the upper one with a scissor-like action to pinch the food between upper and lower tips.

Bad Manners When Using Chopsticks

Mayoi-bashi

Mayoi means "dithering". It is bad manners to wave your chopsticks around aimlessly over the food, trying to decide what to take next.

Sashi-bashi

Sashi means "inserting". It is bad manners to spear food with the points of the chopsticks as if they were a fork.

Yosé-bashi

Yosé means "drawing near". It is bad manners to pull the dishes towards you using the chopsticks. Always pick the dishes up in the hand.

HANDLING DISHES

Japanese dishes are designed to be the right size and shape for holding in the hand. It is a particularly important point of etiquette to lift the dishes to the breast when eating rice or drinking soup.

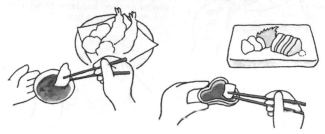

When eating *tempura* (see p. 36), *sashimi* (raw fish) or other food which is dipped in sauce before being eaten, use the hand not holding the chopsticks to hold the dish containing the sauce.

The dishes or plates used for grilled fish are usually too large to pick up, and may be left on the table. When eating *nabemono* (hotpots), transfer a portion from the communal pot to your own small dish and then lift this dish to eat.

175

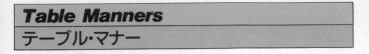

Table Manners
テーブル・マナー

Sit up with your back straight and use your hands and chopsticks to bring the food to the mouth, rather than bending over the table. Tidy up your area of the table when you have finished.

Use your chopsticks to cut up pieces of food too large to fit into the mouth in one bite.

Sip soup and liquid dishes such as *chazuké* (see p. 84) straight from the bowl.

When taking soy sauce, take only the quantity you need, pouring it into the small dish provided for the purpose. It is bad manners to waste it by taking too much.

Tsukemono (pickles) is served in a bowl with an extra pair of chopsticks. So take some onto your plate with those chopsticks. That's formal manners.

When eating *chawan-mushi* (see p. 172) or other food served in bowls with a lid, replace the lid on the bowl when you have finished.

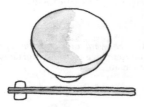

Finish up all the rice in your bowl, down to the last grain.

When eating fish or other food containing bones, leave the bones neatly on the side of the dish.

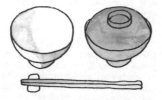

When you have finished your meal, replace your chopsticks tidily on the chopstick rest as they were when you started.

Japanese Tableware
和食器

Japanese plates, bowls, cups and dishes have different shapes depending on the kind of food they are meant to hold. They are also made of a variety of materials, such as earthenware, porcelain, lacquerware, or wood. The great variety of shapes, colors, patterns and materials used in their tableware is evidence that the Japanese regard the presentation and appearance of food as being almost as important as the taste.

Chawan

The *chawan*, or rice bowl, is just the right size to fit comfortably in the hand.

Shiru-wan

The *shiru-wan*, or soup bowl, is for *miso-shiru* (*miso* soup) or *suimono* (clear soup). Most *shiru-wan* are of lacquerware; some have lids, and some do not.

Hashi-oki

The *hashi-oki* (chopstick rest) is used to keep the tips of the chopsticks from coming into contact with the table during pauses in eating.

Yakimono-zara

Literally "dish for grilled things", these dishes are usually rectangular so as to accommodate either whole grilled fish or sliced fish, and come in varying sizes.

Nimono-wan

The *nimono-wan* is a wide-mouthed dish used for boiled and stewed food. It is made of lacquerware or porcelain and comes with or without a lid.

Chūzara and kozara

These medium-sized (*chūzara*) and small (*kozara*) dishes are used for a variety of foods including *sashimi* (raw fish) and *yakimono* (grilled food).

Kobachi

The *kobachi* (small bowl) is used for *sunomono* (vinegared dishes), small quantities of *nimono* (stews), and *chimmi* (special delicacies). Like the *chūzara* and *kozara*, the *kobachi* has a variety of uses.

Domburi-bachi

These large china bowls are used for noodles such as *soba* and *udon*, and for *domburimono* (see p. 72). They come both with and without lids.

Yunomi-jawan

The *yunomi-jawan*, used for green tea, can be small and delicate, or large and sturdy, depending on the occasion and the type of tea being drunk.

Popular Seasonings
テーブル調味料の使い方

All over Japan, people like to season their food with *shōyu* (soy sauce) and *sōsu* (a sauce similar to Worcester sauce). Bottles of these can be found on the dining tables of almost every restaurant and home.

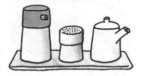

The three most popular seasonings in Japan are *shōyu*, *sōsu*, and salt. The special container used for *shōyu* is called *shōyu-sashi*.

Neri-garashi and neri-wasabi

These little pots contain *neri-garashi* (mustard) and *neri-wasabi* (Japanese horseradish).

Ichimi and shichimi

Ichimi is simply another name for *tōgarashi* (red pepper). *Shichimi* (see p. 94) is a mixture of seven different spices including red pepper.

Koshō

Most of the *koshō* (pepper) used in Japan is already ground, rather than in the form of the peppercorns and grinders popular in the West.

Su (rice vinegar)

All kinds of vinegar are available in Japan, but rice vinegar is used almost exclusively.

Regional Taste Variations
味つけの地方色

Japan is a long, thin country with a great distance between its northernmost and southernmost points, and there are many subtle variations in the seasonings used in cooking from region to region. There is a distinct difference between the food of the Kansai region in the west and the Kantō region, centered around Tōkyō, in the east.

Hokkaidō and Tōhoku

Shōyu (soy sauce)

These are the coldest areas of Japan, and the cooking reflects this, with its liberal use of soy sauce and sugar, and its resulting strong flavoring.

Kyūshū

In this region, as in Okinawa, much of the cooking is based on pork or chicken stock. More sugar is used in cooking in Kyūshū than in the Kantō region.

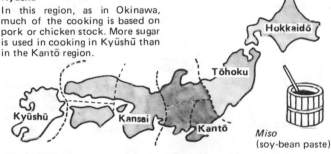

Miso (soy-bean paste)

The Kansai region

Kansai cuisine generally favors a lighter taste based on salt rather than soy sauce. Kansai cooks prefer to retain the natural color of the materials, and do not like the way soy sauce darkens the food.

The Kantō region

Kantō cooking generally has a spicy taste and uses a lot of soy sauce for seasoning. This gives many Kantō dishes a dark color.

Instant Foods & Takeaway Foods
インスタント・テイクアウト食品

More than 50% of Japanese housewives work, so there is a big demand for instant and takeaway foods nowadays.

Kappu-men

A wide variety of instant noodles are sold in food stores and supermarkets. To prepare them, just pour hot water into the large styrofoam cup in which the noodles are sold, and wait for three to five minutes.

Miso-shiru and suimono

Instant *miso-shiru (miso* soup) and *suimono* (clear soup) come in some types. One, for example, is a powder to which hot water must be added, and another is a liquid which must be heated in a pan of hot water.

Retoruto-pakku

Various rice dishes are sold in plastic packages for reheating in hot water. These include plain white rice, and *sekihan* (red rice).

Oshizushi

Ōsakazushi

Unlike *edomaezushi* (see p. 22), *Ōsakazushi* (also called *hakozushi* or *oshizushi*) is made by pressing the rice and fish into wooden molds. It is often sold in supermarkets and department stores.

Onigiri and bentō

Special *bentō* shops selling hot takeaway boxed lunches and *onigiri* (rice balls) have mushroomed in shopping areas and on housing estates in recent years.

Yakitori

Many *yakitori-ya* offer a takeaway service.

Sushi-ori

Sushi restaurants have long offered a takeaway service, packing the *sushi* in a chipbox called *ori*.

INDEX

* Both English and Japanese terms, with the Japanese characters for the latter, are listed in the index below.

E

F

M

N

O

T

英文 **日本絵とき事典 3**

ILLUSTRATED

EATING IN JAPAN

初 版 発 行	1985年3月20日
改 訂 9 版	1993年1月20日
	（Jan.20,1993 9th edition）
編 集 人	甲斐順子
発 行 人	岩田光正
発 行 所	JTB 日本交通公社出版事業局
印 刷 所	交通印刷株式会社

企画・編集	JTB 出版事業局 編集二部
	外語図書編集 担当編集長 黒澤明夫
取材・編集協力	株式会社アーバン・トランスレーション
	越膳百々子・氏家和子
イ ラ ス ト	松下正己・MAJORICA
表紙デザイン	東 芳純
翻 訳	John Howard Loftus

●図書のご注文は
JTB 出版販売センター ☎03-3477-9588
〒150 東京都渋谷区道玄坂1-10-8 渋谷野村ビル7階
●本書の内容のお問合せは
JTB 出版事業局 編集二部 ☎03-3477-9566
〒150 東京都渋谷区道玄坂1-10-8 渋谷野村ビル7階
●広告のお問合せは
JTB 出版事業局 広告部 ☎03-3477-9531

923807 712052
ISBN4-533-00456-3

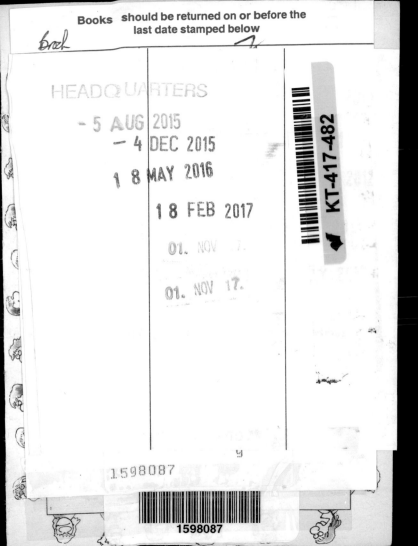

The Vital Spark is an imprint of
Neil Wilson Publishing Ltd
303 The Pentagon Centre
36 Washington Street
GLASGOW
G3 8AZ

Tel: 0141-221-1117
Fax: 0141-221-5363
E-mail: info@nwp.co.uk
www.nwp.co.uk
www.vitalspark.co.uk

ISBN 1-903238-52-8

Typeset in Bodoni
Designed by Mark Blackadder

Printed in Poland

Contents

Part Two
'The Truths Ma Mother Telt Me!'
59

Introduction

Just listen to conversations these days and you'll notice how frequently folk offer up a piece of advice that begins, 'As my mother used to say …'

When I first started collecting Scottish mothers' sayings I found that most of them were wee white lies. Then I realised that all Scottish mothers told porky-pies to their offspring. They have probably been protecting us for centuries with fibs backed up, of course, with their many truthful sayings, and now you probably hear yourself saying them to your own children!

What your mother said really depended on how she was feeling at the time. If she was happy, the family was happy. If she was scunnered, the family was scunnered. And if your father was scunnered … och, so what!

She tied your shoes then taught you how to tie your own. She took pride in all you did. She was someone who encouraged you when others teased you, who appreciated the things that others failed to notice, who gave you security in an insecure world, who sent you to bed at night when you weren't tired and who woke you up in the morning when you were too tired to get up. She kept you warm and safe, but depending on her mood and situation she stretched the truth a tad with all those loving deceptions.

Most of these fibs your mother uttered were designed, or so she thought, to keep us out of harm's way, to preserve the sanctity of our childhood or, when necessary, to give us a boost of confidence as we grew up. It was really a homely form of spin-doctoring as most of them contained only a smidgen of truth. Then there were her other sayings and truths, home-truths, half-truths … all to keep us in line and ensure we grew up safely.

Whether you are a Scot at home or part of the great Caledonian diaspora, we all have one thing in common. We were all trained by our mothers and Scottish mothers just can't help those wee white lies. Indeed in August 2001 a survey commissioned by *That's Life!* magazine found that 99 per cent of Scots-women admit to telling small fibs.

From generation to generation, Scottish mothers have said the same things to their children. It's part of being a mum. Giving birth is the initial thing … then it's the upbringing … looking after the growing chicks. All the well-established maternal clichés and phrases were somehow programmed into mothers, thereby shaping our lives and behaviour by the string of words they continually flung at us. Children need to be loved so that the seeds of self-esteem can grow. But when they overstep the mark mothers must show their disappointment with their behaviour. And we are all really the direct result of our mother's influence along with a mixture of her prejudices and values in life, combined with a fair selection of old-wives tales, common sense … and those little white lies, plus her more truthful sayings!

In reality our mothers were our inspiration. They wanted to guide our behaviour through life. They wanted us to be a credit to them. In fact it is said that no matter how old a Scottish mother gets, she still watches her middle-aged children for signs of improvement! And now when you hear yourself, *it's just your mother talking!*

Part One

'Lies and Truths
Ma Mother Telt Me!'

scunnered

1
Lies to Make You Behave

If you don't behave ah'll pawn ye an' sell the ticket!

I'll chop your heid aff and sew on a button!

Right! Ah'm cancelling Christmas.

A wee birdie told me.

Any more nonsense and you go to Quarriers.
(The Orphanage in Bridge of Weir.)

You'll be the death o' me.

Oor Wullie would never do anything bad like that.

I've got eyes in the back of my head you know.

Any more carry-on and I'll get the driver to
turn this bus around!

Any more carry-on
and I'll get the driver
to turn this bus around

If you don't like this family, go and find
one that'll take you in!

You're driving me tae an early grave!

Don't you dare go down that lane …
that's where the bogeyman lives.

If ye pick dandelions, ye'll pee the bed.

Ye won't be happy 'till ye'r greetin'.

You could swing a monkey aff that petted lip.
(I can see you're in the huff.)

If you're not back into that bed by the time
I count to 10, I'm calling the polis.

Ye've got a face on ye like a nippy-sweety.
(A nippy-sweety is a bitter person.)

Calm down, you're as high as a kite.

10

Yer face looks like a torn melodeon!
(You look upset.)

Just you be careful what you wish for or you'll get
more than you bargained for!

One day your pigeons will come home tae roost.
(One day your actions will impact on you.)

Don't you give me that look. I invented it!

I'll remember this when it comes tae buyin' yer
birthday present!

You'll laugh on the other side of your face in a minute.
(If you don't behave, you'll be sorry.)

Think bad thoughts and God will make it happen.

An' you behave yersel' at the swimming pool.
Don't you dare come back here drooned!

You'll get your heid in yer hauns tae play with.
(Behave … or you'll be sorry.)

If you're not in by nine o'clock Wee
Wully Winkie will get you.

Come here you! I'm all stressed oot wi'
naebuddy tae strangle.

11

I'm going to put every one of your toys
in that dustbin.

If you don't stop arguing I'll shoot the boots off you.

Ah think you were vaccinated wi' a gramophone
needle. (You never seem to stop talking.)

If I had talked to my mother the way you talk to me,
she'd have murdered me.

I don't care what everybody's mothers say …
you're not going.

Listen you! Growing old is unavoidable.
Growing up is optional!

In a minute ah'm gonnae go ma dinger!
(In a minute I'm going to lose my temper.)

I always know what you're up to.

It wid make the cat laugh. (Don't be silly.)

If ah've told ye once ah've told you a million times …

If you eat the last slice you'll end up an old maid.

If ye died wi' a face like that naebuddy wid wash it.
(For goodness sake, smile.)

Don't stick out that tongue or ye'll trip o'er it.

Don't stare or yer eyes will stick.

The only reason ah'm nice tae you is so ye'll
visit me in the old folks' home.

I'm talking tae a brick wall.

I'm not as green as I'm cabbage-looking.
(Do you think I'm daft?)

13

If you give me another dirty
look yer face will look like last year's rhubarb.

If you don't stop crossing yer eyes,
they're going to stay that way.

You can't fool me. I'm yer mother!

Ladies never say bad words.

That tongue o' yours is that
sharp ye'll cut yersel'.

Ye've goat a face on ye
like a Corporation bus.
(What's the matter with you?)

Close that door! Yur heatin'
the whole o' Scotland.

2
Lies about Your body

You can have your ears pierced when you're 14.

Don't be silly. All clever people have big ears.

Yawning gives you spotty cheeks.

You got that special birthmark so you'll
never need a tattoo.

Sometimes you've goat a face on ye like a
well-skelped bum. (For goodness sake, cheer up.)

If your nose itches someone is coming.

You're wee because you were such a clever baby
and I kept patting you on yer heid.

Eat your crusts and you'll get curly hair.

Straighten that face; if the wind changes
it'll stay like that.

Ye've got a face on ye like the far end o' a
French fiddle. (You look as though you're
just about to whine.)

Don't be silly, moles are beauty spots.

LODGER'S ARMS

Keep yer arms tucked in in bed or ye'll get a reach
like a lodger. (Lodgers had a reputation for
stretching for extras during the meal.)

If you've a dimple on yer chin,
you're a wee devil within.

If you keep biting these nails a finger
will grow in your stomach.

Brush your hair at night and you'll forget the
bad things that happened during the day.

Yer hair's like straw hingin' oot a midden.

Yer lang and wee, like the cat's elbow.
(You're too thin.)

All boys prefer girls who are wee.

There must be billions of germs crawling
over that filthy neck.

Ye look like ye fell oot the ugly tree and
hit every branch on the way doon.
(Go and tidy yourself up.)

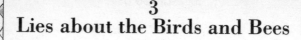

3
Lies about the Birds and Bees

You're a good-lookin' wee thing. Ye'll need
tae keep baith legs in the wan stockin'.

Ah'll tell ye aboot it soon.

If he doesn't understand 'no', explain it
with wi' yer elbows.

If you keep touching yourself you'll go blind.

If you sit on a public loo seat, you'll get pregnant.

The nurse brought you in her wee black bag.

Yer belly button is where the angels
poked at ye to see if you were done.

Girls like boys who wear ties.

All good girls wait.

A baby is a bit of stardust blown
out of God's hand.

Why should a farmer buy a cow
when he can get his milk free?
(Wait till you're married.)

It would kill your father.

Men don't show their feelings.

Ye'll be an old maid if ye wait fur the hats
while the bunnets pass bye.
(You can wait a long time and never
find the ideal man.)

Yer not complete until ye make me a granny.

You can change him.

You'll never change him.

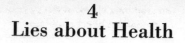

4
Lies about Health

Castor oil cures everything but a widden leg.

Get it doon ye. It'll do ye good.

Don't sniff or it'll gum up yer belly button.

You only get beauty sleep afore midnight.

You'll get cross-eyed if you pee outside.

If ye wet the bed the fairy underneath will drown.

Wash yer neck. That's jist a cat's lick.
(You've hardly washed yourself.)

If you step on a crack in the pavement
yer faither'll get chilblains.

Wash yer hands afore ye eat or
you'll get bed-bugs.

If you pull out a hair seven others
will go to its funeral.

You don't need to brush all yer teeth.
Jist the wans ye want tae keep.

If you pick your nose your head will cave in.

Yer like a Scotch warming pan.
(You're running a temperature. It is said that in
some Scottish mansions a servant was often put
in the bed to warm in up for the Laird!)

If you touch a frog you get warts.

Only spit would get a dirty face like that clean.
(Your face is absolutely filthy!)

Yawning without covering your mouth gives
you pimples.

If you wear a hat in the house you get a headache.

Always wash between your toes or
turnips will grow there.

Always wash behind your ears or
tatties will grow there.

If you don't chew your food
40 times you get worms.

Don't brush your hair into a bun or a wee bird
will come and make its nest there.

You've got a sore throat because you don't
wear your gloves.

If you suck your thumb you'll get boils.

If ye whistle in the hoose,
yer hair will stop growing.

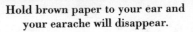

Hold brown paper to your ear and
your earache will disappear.

If you sit around in a wet bathing suit
you get ingrowing toenails.

What doesn't kill you makes
you stronger.

The worse it tastes the better it does you.

Put a button in the wrong buttonhole
and you get sore ears.

The crust of the loaf has all the goodness.

Eating bananas when you have your
period gives you cramp.

It's better for your health if you
sit on the floor.

Whistling in the house gives you
hairs on your chin.

If you touch a plant during
your period it'll die.

5
Lies about Spiritual Matters

God will punish you for this.

Sneezing is the wind off the devil's wings.

Salt and vinegar keep the devil away.

Always polish an apple before you eat it.
That'll keep the angels happy.

Heaven and Hell ain't what they used
to be when I was young.

If someone says, 'Hell', you must turn around
seven times and knock on wood.

6
Lies during the Teenage Years

No, I wasn't listening in to your call.
I was just trying to phone granny.

Ye look as though ye've been dragged
through a hedge backwards.

Don't be silly, I didn't stay up.
I was watching a video.

Yer as auld fashioned as tea.

Yer no' goin' oot wearing that skirt.
It's like two duck eggs in a hankie.
(Your skirt is too across your bottom.)

You're a wonderful singer.

You look like a deserter oot a kirkyard.

Yer heid's full o' mince.

Well, you have to suffer to be beautiful.

You look like something the cat dragged in.

You're too auld fashioned for your age.

No, I wasn't looking through your drawers.
I was just puffing away your clean underwear.

Ye look like wan o'clock half struck!
(You've not wakened up yet.)

Him. He's as common as muck!

Get that make-up off. Ye've goat
a face oan ye like a raw dumplin'.

7
Lies about Marriage

Eat a tomato on your wedding day
and you'll have twins.

Marry at the full moon and you
get water on the brain.

Sex isnae fun unless you're married.

No-one on my side of the family
has ever had to get married.

Your faither and I never argue.

Your faither's o'er deef an' ah'm half-blind,
an' that's why we're happy.

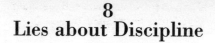

8
Lies about Discipline

If you don't clean under
that bed the duke will pay us a visit.

You heard me fine. All the weans in the
street came in for their tea but you.

Big boys don't cry.

Big girls don't cry.

I'm doing this for your own good.

Because I'm your mother, that's why!

Just wait 'til your faither gets home.

What did yer last servant die of?

That's as clear as mud.

Yer that far ahead o' yersel' ye'll meet
yersel' comin' back.
(You are assuming too much.)

Wait till I get you hame!

Ye'll only get it when a coo calves a cuddie.
(You're never going to get it.)

If you're trying to drive me crazy you're too late.

Yer jist opening yer mouth an' lettin'
yer belly rumble.

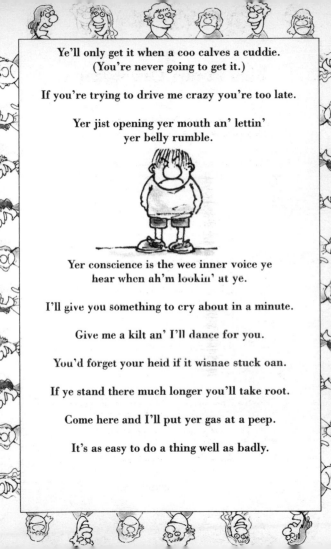

Yer conscience is the wee inner voice ye
hear when ah'm lookin' at ye.

I'll give you something to cry about in a minute.

Give me a kilt an' I'll dance for you.

You'd forget your heid if it wisnae stuck oan.

If ye stand there much longer you'll take root.

Come here and I'll put yer gas at a peep.

It's as easy to do a thing well as badly.

9
Lies about the House

What happened to your
bedroom floor? I can't find it.

Don't open an umbrella in the house.
It'll bring bad luck.

Whistling in the house encourages mice.

If you don't clean that nose
we'll have a visitor soon.

If I come into that room and find it,
there'll be big trouble!

It's like Charing Cross at
the rush hour in this hoose.

Ok. So, Mr Nobody did that?

There'll be new rules from
now on in this house!

If you came in by the front door,
leave by the back.

Never hand me a knife.
Put it on the table so that I can pick it up.

Don't put shoes on a table top.
It's bad luck.

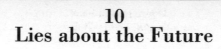

10
Lies about the Future

Jist remember. In life wan minute you're a peacock
an' the next you're a feather duster.

When you're all grown-up,
you can sit in the front seat.

When you have a house I'll come and
see if you're keeping it clean.

You can catch more flies with honey than with vinegar.
(It's better to be diplomatic than aggressive.)

It's unlucky to start a job on a Wednesday.

Your opinion doesn't count unless you're grown-up.

Just wait. Your kids will drive you crazy the
way you're driving me crazy.

Whit gangs roon, comes aroon.

You'll be rich because you were born
on a bank holiday.

Don't let yersel' go tae the pigs and whistles.
(Keep up your standards in life.)

**Don't go on a boat
on a Sunday or you'll drown.**

Going to work is great fun.

Once ye've made yer bed, ye'll need tae lie in it.

33

11
Lies about the Weather

There's enough blue sky tae mak a sailor's breeks.
(It's a beautiful day.)

'guid clean drizzle'

Ye've been raised in
nothing but guid, clean drizzle.
(I've given you my best.)

Thunder is jist God playing at bowls.

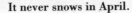

It never snows in April.

So it's raining. You're no' sugar.
You'll no disappear.

If it wis raining palaces
you'd get hit wi' a dunnie door!
Note: A dunnie is a basement.

Lightning is God jist being a wee bit angry.

Rain is jist the angels crying.

It's raining cats and dogs out there.

All good children wear a trenchcoat.

12
Lies to Preserve Our Inocence

Your faither and I were getting married onyway.

Of course fairies are real. If you don't believe
in them, some poor wee fairy will die.

Your teddy with the one eye has
gone to live in heaven.

An' whit I say had better no' leave this hoose
or ah'll chop that tongue off!

There's the wee man in the
moon looking down, so be good!

Look. Santa has eaten up
the biscuits you left for him.

Don't go near that water by yourself.
The Loch Ness Monster might get you.

Put your tooth under your pillow.
If you are good the tooth fairy will take it
and leave you sixpence.

And they lived happily ever after.

Look at a star and make a wish
and it'll come true.

Too much kissing can make you pregnant.

If you go out looking like that
you'll end up pregnant.

Bite your tongue and what you've
said won't come true.

13
Lies about Lying

People believe anything if you whisper.

I would never even tell you a teeny, weeny lie.

I crossed my fingers so that wee fib didn't count.

See! God gave you these hiccups for telling a lie.

Your father and I never tell lies.

Ah never blaw in yer lug.
(I never flatter or deceive you.)

You get a black spot on your tongue when you tell lies.

Mothers can always tell when you're lying.

You get pimples on your bum when you lie.

14
Lies about School

Of course everybody will have their schoolbooks covered in wallpaper!

If you don't get dressed then you can go to school in your pyjamas.

Algebra is easy.

Just ignore that bully and he/she'll stop.

That blazer makes you look very attractive.

During an exam pull on your ear
and you'll remember what you studied.

Sticks and stones will break your bones
but names will never hurt you.

Wait and see. Next week
you'll both be best friends.

Homework can be great fun.

I think you were behind the barn door
when they were giving oot brains.

15
Reassuring Lies

Your faither would make
mincemeat o' him.

I didn't read your diary.
I was just tidying it away.

Freckles are just God's kisses.

Don't worry. There's only a couple of days
between a good haircut and a bad one.

Someday you'll thank me for this.

Och, it's jist a wee scratch.

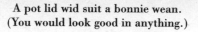

A pot lid wid suit a bonnie wean.
(You would look good in anything.)

Everything happens for a reason.

We're almost there.

It's jist a phase you're going through.

If you get your Highers you'll
never be unemployed.

Miracles happen all the time.

You're all there and back again.
(You're really smart)

Anyway, you've a nice personality.

No news is good news.

You can only see it in the light.

Nobody will ever notice.

You're as cute as a new pin.

It's perfect. Just what I wanted.

Don't worry dear. You'll fill out.

It'll look better when it's pressed.

They were the dearest
glasses in the opticians.

It will look better when your
hair grows in again.

You're as cute as a dumplin' in a hankie.

Looks aren't everything.

If it doesn't have teeth it won't bite you.

He's not the only fish in the sea.

It's just baby fat, silly.

You're nae different frae onybuddy else.

Nobody will ever notice.

It's perfect. Just what you needed.

43

16
Lies about Birth and Death

Washing babies' hands washes away
their good fortune.

If you watch someone until they are
out of sight, they never come back alive.

If there is a full moon at Christmas the
cemetery will be busy in January.

All deaths happen in threes.

Don't be silly, I won't die for another 50 years.

Grandma asked for you at the end.

You cover the mirrors in the house
so their souls won't stay.

Don't point in a cemetery or you're
finger will turn green.

He looks as though he has
one foot in the grave and the
other on a banana skin.

God always taks the best
fur himsel'.

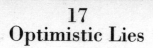

17
Optimistic Lies

Everything always works out for the best.

It's never too late for anything.

There's a place for everything and
everything has its place.

Good things happen to good people.

It's never, ever too late.

You can change the world.

It's not often you're wrang, but ye'r right again.

18
Lies about Money

The money man's deed.

If you only marry for money you will earn it.

Fools an' their money are soon partying.

Money is something I never think about.

I bought it because it's ideal for you.
Not because it was in a sale.

They're as poor as dirt.

Carnegie's yer uncle.

You think money grows on trees.

If your right hand palm itches you're just about to get money. If your left one itches you'll get a bill.

Money burns a hole in your pocket.

IT'S A BANK MANAGER!

Your fists were closed when you were born. That's why you're mean.

You throw money around like a man wi' nae arms.

What's yours is mine and what's mine's ma own.

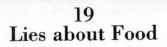

19
Lies about Food

All the other boys and girls in your
class will be eating their broccoli

Eating carrots is good for your eyesight.

If you eat a raw potato you get worms.

No, I didn't deliberately eat
your sweets. I was just making sure
they were suitable for you.

Your eyes are bigger than your belly.

Ah'm that hungry ah could
eat a scabby-heedid horse.

Eating Brussel sprouts
makes you good-looking.

Butter doesn't stick tae your bread.
(You're an unlucky person.)

Cutting the loaf from both ends brings bad luck.

Eat up your cabbage. After a while
it tastes like chocolate.

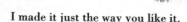

I made it just the way you like it.

Ye'r as greedy as ten cocks scrapping a
midden for a barley pickle.

If you drink straight from the bottle
you get willie-wobbles.

Get it down you. You don't know what you're missing.

Pepper without salt gives you fever.

If you talk with your mouth full a fly will get in.

Fish helps your brain. If you ate some you'd
maybe know what I was talking about.

It's as plain as purridge.

Eat up. It's charity week at the b'roo.
(Let's enjoy ourselves regardless of the cost.
Note: the 'b'roo' was the job centre.)

20
Lies about Herself

I was just away to see a man about a dog.

When I think of what I sacrificed to get
you those piano lessons.

I'm making a New Year resolution to stop smoking.

Of course I'm listening to you.
I *always* listen to everything you say.

I voted while you were at school.

No, I haven't started smoking again.
They're my friend's cigarettes.

God bless my bloomers!

I'm all in apart from the soles of my shoes.
(I'm exhausted.)

I *do* feel bad about it.

I worked for this. I owe it to myself.

I'm not 40. If anyone asks
say you don't know.

Of course I was a virgin
when I married dad.

I *am* listening to you.

And here's me workin' ma
fingers to the bone.

I'm not sick. Just tired.

I only smoke to let you see how bad
it is for your chest.

I very seldom go out.

I don't remember a thing about that.

I understand you completely.

I always listen to your opinions.

I've been cooking all day for you.

I did give up smoking. It's just that
it didn't give me up.

Don't do as I do. Do as I say.

It's only yer mother that's going to tell
you the truth in this life.

Not that ah'm wan tae talk about
onybuddy else, but …

53

21
Lies about Clothes

Don't be silly, it's lovely. Sure, it was one of your big sister's favourite dresses.

You'll grow into it.

It looks better on you than it did on your sister.

Look. Now you're a trendsetter.

Blue is your best colour.

It's back in fashion now.

It's never really been out of fashion, has it?

Don't put your shoes on a chair. It'll bring bad luck.

Everyone is wearing purple.

It fits perfectly.

22
Lies about Pets

Goldfish can be just as friendly as dogs.

If you give wee Sandy your dinner
you'll need to eat his.

No, you're not getting a hampster.
Your father is allergic to them.

Dog's breath melts your bones.

There's more than one way to skin a cat.

It was the dog who let-off!

Scratch a dog where it
can't scratch and it will
never run away.

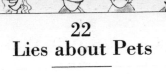

We can't have a cat. Your wee sister
is frightened of them.

What do you want a dog for?
You've got a wee brother.

Your wee kitten got sick so we sent
her back to her mummy and daddy.

23
Lies about the Family

If you step on a nail, your faither's in jail.

Your wee brother didn't hit you.
These were just love pats.

Bachelors' wives and auld maids' bairns are aye well bred. (Her answer to those within the family who gave advice on matters of which they had no experience.)

Your brothers and sisters are your very best friends.

Blood is thicker than water.

Yer uncle's all there and back again.
(He's shrewd.)

Your brother was asking for you when he phoned.

That wean's been here before.
(What a mature child.)

Yer Auntie's mair tae be
pitied than laughed at.

Mean! She widnae gae ye
the skin aff her custard.

Dogs bark as they are bred.

All your good points come from my
side of the family.

Your father always has a good
reason for everything he does.

24
Lies about the
'Good Old Days'

Your grandfather never touched strong drink.

I only got an apple for my Christmas.

The outside toilet was three stairs
down and used by 30 families.

I had to walk 10 miles to school every day.

Were we poor? You don't know the half of it!

Part Two

'The Truths Ma Mother Telt Me!'

And then there was the other stuff ... the truths, sayings, orders and cajoling.

You see, mothers have the responsibility of getting their offspring to wash, go to bed, then get out of bed, get dressed, have breakfast, go off to school and so on and so forth in a never-ending cycle. She must have half-a-dozen hands, be able to put three children on her knees at the one time, and have a kiss that can cure anything from a sore leg to a broken heart. To the world a mother might seem as one person, but to one person she may just be the world.

In the absence of a sheepdog she has to round up, threaten and use all her ingenuity to continually go through this series of events, whilst knocking her children into shape to become reasonably responsible citizens through her encouragement and words of wisdom. An almost impossible task really, but, as we know, mothers usually manage it in the end.

25
Being Wary in Life

Watch out. There's many a
barber would shave a beardless man.

What the devil can't do he gets others to do.

Every man's nose winna be a shoeing horn.
(Some things can only be used for one purpose.)

Before you open your mouth ask yourself,
will the words be kind, true and necessary?

Beg frae beggars and you'll ne'er be rich.
(Pick good friends.)

The rabbit's foot didnae work for the rabbit.

Never do anything I wouldn't do.

Yer thoughts are your own, but yer words are not.

Only mothers' hugs are free.

Further east, the shorter west.
(There are always two ways to look at things.)

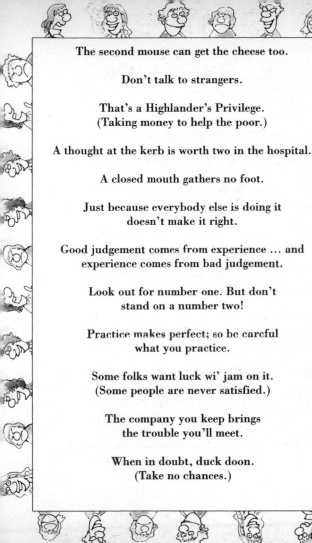

The second mouse can get the cheese too.

Don't talk to strangers.

That's a Highlander's Privilege.
(Taking money to help the poor.)

A thought at the kerb is worth two in the hospital.

A closed mouth gathers no foot.

Just because everybody else is doing it
doesn't make it right.

Good judgement comes from experience ... and
experience comes from bad judgement.

Look out for number one. But don't
stand on a number two!

Practice makes perfect; so be careful
what you practice.

Some folks want luck wi' jam on it.
(Some people are never satisfied.)

The company you keep brings
the trouble you'll meet.

When in doubt, duck doon.
(Take no chances.)

Something for nothing is like a worm.
It's usually got a hook in it.

Watch out. Bad luck takes no holidays.

Better to be ill-spoken of by one before all,
than by all afore one.

Ye cannae get the whole truth into one sentence.

An opinion is only bettered by the
facts that support it.

All sins cast long shadows.

Don't fly with the owls at
night and the sparrows by day.

Never say all you think.

Drink nothing without seeing it.
Sign nothing without reading it.

Let folks know what you stand for,
and what you won't stand for.

Drugs is for mugs.

If the shoe fits, wear it.

Treat others as they should treat you.

Watch out who you sit next
to on trains and buses.

Avoid evil and it should avoid you.

Use yer savvy. Common sense is a gift.

There are three rules to getting on in life:
Improve. Improve. Improve.

Words are wind, but
seeing's believing.

26
Being Sensible

Use it up, wear it out,
make it do or do without.

Never burn your quilt because of the fleas.
(Don't take unnecessary actions.)

One hand can't wash itself.
(It is better to work as a team.)

Don't buy hay for a house that's not yours.
(Your priority is first to yourself.)

Don't cross the river to get water.

Wise folks never blow their own nose.
(It is better that other people say nice
things about you rather than yourself.)

Think twice afore ye say no.

Luck only lends; it never gives.
(You can't expect to be lucky all of the time.)

Behave. Don't be a right chookie.
(Don't act like a brainless hen.)

It's a long road for a shortcut.
(There's a better way of doing this.)

Dinna stretch yer arm further than
yer sleeve'll let ye. (Don't overdo things.)

Ask a question and be a fool for two minutes.
Don't ask and be a fool for life.

Never be too proud to ask for help.

Better you laugh than I greet.
(It's better to be laughed at for not doing something,
than doing it and be sorry for it.)

Is that just a think or is it a know?
(Are you really sure of what you just said?)

Don't show yer dragged-up-ness.

You don't get rid of your temper by losing it.

Better wan eye than hail blin'.

Advice is least heeded when it's most needed.

Facts are chiels that winna ding!
(You can't argue with the facts.)

If the whole street believe something stupid,
it's still stupid.

Always control your senses because you
can't control your thoughts.

If it quacks like a duck, walks like a duck
and looks like a duck – it's a duck.

Never bother trouble till trouble bothers you.

Ye cannae tak the breeks aff a Hielandman!
(You can't take something from someone
who doesn't possess it.)

Don't learn to shave on another man's chin.
(Try things out for yourself.)

Folks make their own luck.

Experience is something you get when
you don't want it.

Wait till night afore ye say it's
been a grand day.

A clear conscience maks a soft pillow.

Hae some haud in yer haun.
(Don't be a spendthrift.)

Gey the Lord's leather tae the Lord's weather.
(It's a nice day and you don't need
to wear so much.)

Of all ills, nane's best.

27
Hygiene – Etiquette – Tidiness

Is that hanky clean?

Horses sweat, men perspire and ladies glow.

Favours unused are favours abused.

Never drink out your saucer.

Ye brush up well.

If you can't say something nice, say nothing.

Be true to your teeth or they'll be false to you.

Don't you dare use that sleeve as a hankie.

Straighten that back.

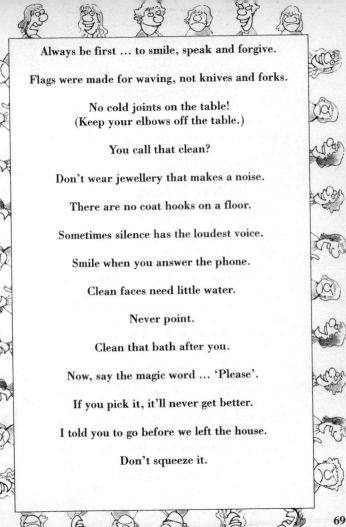

Always be first ... to smile, speak and forgive.

Flags were made for waving, not knives and forks.

No cold joints on the table!
(Keep your elbows off the table.)

You call that clean?

Don't wear jewellery that makes a noise.

There are no coat hooks on a floor.

Sometimes silence has the loudest voice.

Smile when you answer the phone.

Clean faces need little water.

Never point.

Clean that bath after you.

Now, say the magic word ... 'Please'.

If you pick it, it'll never get better.

I told you to go before we left the house.

Don't squeeze it.

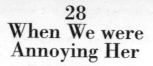

28

When We were
Annoying Her

Who's kidding who? The dog did not do that!

Don't call me 'she'. I'm yer mother.

There'll be tears afore bedtime.

Because I said so. That's why!

Has the cat got yer tongue?

You'll be sorry when I'm dead and gone.

If ye had given sixpence for that word,
    ye widna hae used it.

Just wait 'til you have children of your own.

Was that funny ha ha or funny peculiar?

I'm no' asking you. I'm telling you!

You jist talk frae the teeth forward.

(You speak with your lips but not with your heart.)

If I wanted backchat I'd have bought a parrot.

Ah think you're pulling ma chain.

And another thing ... I'll be your mother
till the day I die.

Aye, ye think yer nae sma' drink.
(You really think you're something special.)

As long as you live under my roof you'll do as I do.

I'm going to give you until I
count to three. One ... two ...

Away tae Hecklebirnie!
(Only said when she was really fed up with you.
It is a place three miles beyond hell!)

You've always got to have
an answer for everything,
haven't you?

You're going to poke yer eye out
with that thing. (Be careful!)

Listen! In this house push
yer belly button for service. If
ah don't answer, do it yersel'.

Stop yer girnin'.

You've only got a clear conscience because
you've got a bad memory.

Ah dinny lift ye afore ye fa'.
(I never find fault with you until you
give me good cause.)

How many times have I got to tell you …?

Dae ye think ma heid buttons up the back?
and
Dae ye think ah came up the Clyde oan a bike?
(Do you think I'm daft?)

If you don't come when I call you it
will save you coming back.

Pride's an ill horse tae ride.

After all the things I've done for you.

Yer tongue might not weigh much,
but you cannae hold it.

'M' stands for mother … no' maid!

Well, you can jist stick that in yer pipe and smoke it.

I said maybe, and that's final.

If I catch you doing that one more time …

I'll give ye something tae greet for.

How dare you stop me when I'm interrupting.

For you 'no' is a complete sentence.

Stop ringing that clapper!
(Hold your tongue!)

The first step to wisdom is keeping quiet.
The second is listening.

Dae ye think ah'm daft jist because ah slaver
at the mooth?

What part of 'no' don't you understand?

Half a tale is enough for a wise man.

Don't you dare roll those eyes at me.

Ye've a guid Scotch tongue in yer heid –
if ye speak ah'll answer.

I'll gae ye wan and lend ye another!)
(Do you want a smacking?)

You've given me a bonny blue nothing wi'
a whistle on the top.

Can youse no' take a tellin'?

Barrows don't move unless ye gae them a shove.
(You have to act, not just talk.)

29
Keeping Us out of Mischief

There's nothing you can't do after midnight
you can't do before midnight. So you'll be
home here by midnight.

If you give people your tuppenceworth
you might just get some change.
(If you are frank with people you might
just get more than you bargained for.)

You do that and ah'll be black affronted.
(Don't make me ashamed of you.)

Don't be a two-legged cratur wi'
a goose's heid an' a hen's heart.
(Don't be a foolish coward.)

I don't care who started it. I'm finishing it!

Your true character comes out in the dark.

Don't do anything I wouldn't do,
and that gives you plenty of scope.

And just remember, you're known
by the company you keep.

Watch that tongue. It's wet and keeps slipping.

I'll start treating you like an adult
when you start acting like one.

If you win at that you'll lose at naething.
(You're doing something wrong and it will be
to your disadvantage in the long run.)

30
When She was Proud of Us

Yer a right wee bobby-dazzler.
(You're just great!)

Remember. A pat on the heid is only
inches fae a smack on the bum.

You're a wee stoatir.
(You're terrific.)

When I count my blessings I count
you twice … sometimes!

Huggin's a great gift.

If ye were chocolate I'd eat ye!

Huv a wee coorie-in, pet.
(Let's have a snuggle.)

You were the best looking wee
tottie baby in the hospital.

Ah'm fair
taken wi' you.
(I'm proud of you.)

31
Material Possessions

Whit ye've never had, ye'll never miss.

Ah don't care if everybody else has
one ... you're no' getting' one!

It's not what you wear, it's who you are.

Keep some money in your mattress to fall back on!

Don't spend yer money on things you don't
need just to impress folks you don't like.

If you're content with nothing you possess everything.

The most important things in life aren't 'things'.

Don't discuss money with strangers.

Only fools think that value and
price are the same thing.

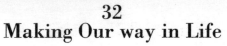

32
Making Our way in Life

Sticks and stones'll break your bones
but names will never hurt you.

What's for ye will no' go by ye.

There's no disgrace in falling down.
The disgrace is lying there.

Don't start anything you don't plan to finish.

Treat your friends like family,
and you family like friends.

Guid folks hae costly names.
(Good reputations have to be earned.)

Only worry tomorrow.

Always do right. It'll please some
folks and astonish others.

Hope and health are brothers.

Hard work's no' easy.

Everybody smiles in the same language.

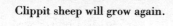

Clippit sheep will grow again.

What may be done anytime will be done at no time.
(Don't procrastinate.)

The best way to look good is to feel good!

If you want a friend, be a friend.

Do weel and dread nae shame.
(Just do your best.)

Smile when you lose. But see next time … win!

Look at the sunshine and others will follow.

Talking o'er much keeps you deaf.

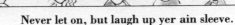

Never let on, but laugh up yer ain sleeve.

Tarry Lang brought little hame.
(Don't waste time.)

Live and let live is what I say.

Early sow, early mow.

To make your dreams come true you
have to stay awake.

If you chase two mice you don't catch any.

Preparation improves luck.

If you fail to prepare, prepare to fail.

Ye've got to do your own growing regardless
of yer faither's height.

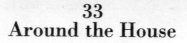

33
Around the House

If you're not in bed by the time
I count to 20 you're in big trouble.

Just one drink of water.
And see if you wet that bed ...!

Quiet! I can't hear myself think!

... and if I hear another peep out of you ...

Doesn't anybody know how to turn
off a light in this house?

Sleep tight. Don't let the bed bugs bite.

Don't you dare wipe those hands on
the towel till they're clean.

You can look but don't touch.

East, west, hame's best.

Houses are made with bricks.
Homes are made with love.

When there's anything to be done in this
house you're away like snow aff a dyke.
(You always disappear when there's work to be done.)

Wishes don't wash dishes.

Don't put that near your mouth.
You don't know where it's been.

I thought I told you to start getting ready for bed.

I heard your alarm clock from the kitchen
and here you are still sleeping.

Eat up. Yer at yer auntie's.

What are you doing up at 11 o'clock.

It's way past your bedtime.

When was the last time
you made that bed.

Close that door. You'd think
you were born in a barn.

Cracked bells never mend.
(Throw that thing out.
You'll never get it repaired.)

This place looks like a pig-sty.

Yer faither's got his ain back teeth.
(Your father is not a fool.)

That's Jock's news.
(I've heard that story before.)

34
Food

Tae hang wi' poverty.
Pit another pea in the soup.

Think of all the starving children in Africa.

Don't you dare turn up your nose at my food!

If you indulge, you bulge.

How do you know you don't like it
when you haven't even tried it?

A dug wi' a bone kens nae freens.
(Not all of that food is just for you.)

If you leave anything on your
plate you'll get if for breakfast.

Dinnae eat cake tae save the bread.
(Get your priorities right.)

You've goat a choice today.
Take it or leave it.

No pudding for you tonight
and don't say I didn't warn you.

OK. Who put their finger in
the condensed milk?

Better to wait on the
cook than the doctor.
(Don't be so impatient
for your meal.)

35
The Opposite Sex

What does his father do?

Many a person has been stung by a little honey.

Better half-hanged than ill-married.

Cocks might crow but hens deliver.
(It's the women who do all the work around here.)

Never let a fool kiss you,
and never let a kiss fool you!

Better nae man than an ill man.

His absence is guid company.
(You're better off without him.)

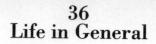

36
Life in General

A giggle a day keeps the glums away.

Ah might be gettin' on but old brushes
know the corners.

Do it now. Then it's done.

Ah forgot tae worry aboot that.

Wanting is not happiness.

Children are poor folks' riches … well, some are!

Hit it wi' a tattie!
(That's posh!)

Happiness can be thought, taught and
caught but not bought.

Ye stand as near the barn door as
makes nae difference. (You're almost related.)

Empty heids are worse than empty pockets.

Sometimes even a blind squirrel finds a nut.

Learn from others' mistakes ... not your own.

If you really want to do something you'll find a way.
If you don't you'll find an excuse.

Things are always better come the morn.

The only things children pass on are their
mother's age and chickenpox.

After all is said and done, usually
more is said than done.

89

We're all stones from
the same mountain.

Ye cannae buy wisdom and health.

Every day comes but once.

Life's like a mirror. You get the
best results when you smile.

Play the cards life deals you.
There are no reshuffles.

Keep laughter up yer jooks.

Every law wis once jist an opinion.

Belittle others, belittle yourself.

Never say, 'if only'.

37
About Herself

Ah'm fair dumfoonert.
(I'm dumbfounded.)

Listen. Us mothers walk in when the
rest of the world walks out.

Yer age is only important if ye're
a cheese.

Ah'm the same age as ma pinkie,
but ma teeth are younger.

When the tea's no' ready, they're
under yer feet. When the tea's on the table,
they're playin' in the street.

Ah never died a winter yet.
(We keep on going regardless.)

Black bum said the pot
tae the cauldron.

Ah've twa holes in ma heid, an' as mony windows.

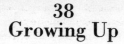

38
Growing Up

Don't keep asking me
questions if you can't live with ma answers.

Give an' take might be the rule in this
house, but ah've taken as much as ah can frae you.

You don't ruin your eyes if you look on the
bright side.

Think the truth, speak the truth and act the truth.

That's the hair o' yer neck.
(That's your weak point/Achilles heel.)

When they're wee they're never aff yer knee.
When they're auld they're never aff yer back.

Pick your friends ... but not to pieces.

Make sure you've on clean
underwear in case you're in an accident.

Call that a dress?
Ye may as well go oot in the bare scuddie.

Only tight shoes make you forget your problems.
(You need something to take your
mind off your concerns.)

A son is a son till he gets a wife,
but a daughter's a daughter all of her life.

Every man blows his ain horn best.

Affront yer pals in daffin', and tine them in earnest.
(Don't offend your friends in jest,
or you may just lose them.)

The best thing you can give your
brother is a good example.

Ye're the bees' knees!

If you go out after I've told you not to then don't
bother coming back – that door will be locked!

The days never know what the years teach.

How many days have
you worn these socks?

Do better today than you did yesterday.

Reputations are made by many
actions and lost by one.

Better tae be oot the world than oot o' fashion.

He that buys land, buys stanes;
he that buys beef, buys banes;
he that buys nuts, buys shells;
he that buys ale, buys naething!

39
Spirituality

God doesn't pay you every month.
He pays you at the end.

If you see a sunset remember whom to thank.

Enjoy life.
Ye'r a lang time deid.

Auld Nick throws
loaded dice. (The devil's
always up to his tricks.)

The hereafter comes not yet.
(Get on with your life.)

Never take away hope from anyone.

Relax on Sundays ... God did.

Night always ends, dawn always comes,
the sun always rises. (Things always improve.)

Things maun aye be someway.
(Be philosophical about life.)

Ye cannae shove yer granny aff a bus!
(There are certain things in life you
can't or shouldn't do.)

40
School

Aye, ye'll go … an' wi' yer lip trimblin'.
(You'll go regardless of how you feel.)

If you're really sick you will stay in
bed all day. But no records, radio or TV.

What do you mean you got *nothing* in school today?

Learning is a treasure you never lose.

You're not getting out to play until
that homework is finished.

So what if you were last in the race,
at least you finished the course.